Degrees and Pedigrees

Degrees and Pedigrees

The Education of America's Top Executives

Michael T. Nietzel

ROWMAN & LITTLEFIELD
Lanham • Boulder • New York • London

Published by Rowman & Littlefield
A wholly owned subsidiary of The Rowman & Littlefield Publishing Group, Inc.
4501 Forbes Boulevard, Suite 200, Lanham, Maryland 20706
www.rowman.com

Unit A, Whitacre Mews, 26-34 Stannary Street, London SE11 4AB

British Library Cataloguing in Publication Information Available

Library of Congress Cataloging-in-Publication Data

Names: Nietzel, Michael T., author.
Title: Degrees and pedigrees : the education of America's top executives / Michael T.
  Nietzel.
Description: London ; New York : Rowman & Littlefield International, [2017] | Includes
  bibliographical references.
Identifiers: LCCN 2017013906 (print) | LCCN 2017032579 (ebook) |
  ISBN 9781475837094 (Electronic) | ISBN 9781475837070 (cloth : alk. paper) |
  ISBN 9781475837087 (pbk. : alk. paper)
Subjects: LCSH: Chief executive officers—Education (Higher—United States. |
  Public officers—Education (Higher—United States. | Universities and colleges—
  United States—Evaluation.
Classification: LCC HD38.25.U6 (ebook) | LCC HD38.25.U6 N54 2017 (print) | DDC
  338.092/273—dc23
LC record available at https://lccn.loc.gov/2017013906

∞™ The paper used in this publication meets the minimum requirements of American
National Standard for Information Sciences—Permanence of Paper for Printed Library
Materials, ANSI/NISO Z39.48-1992.

Printed in the United States of America

Contents

Preface

The idea for this book began in 2005. I had just started my job as president of Missouri State University and was making one of my first road trips to meet with friends and alumni of the university. My destination was Bentonville, Arkansas, where I was to visit former Walmart CEO David Glass, who at the time of our meeting had transitioned to the position of chair of the executive committee of Walmart's Board of Directors. Glass had graduated from what was then Southwest Missouri State University in 1960. Today, Glass Hall is the home of Missouri State's College of Business.

I met Mr. Glass in his office, located in the plain, one-story building that housed most of Walmart's executives. His own office was tiny, almost bare of any decoration, and furnished with a metal desk that was mismatched with a couple of straight-back chairs. I will never forget asking him if all the Walmart offices were like this one, to which he replied, "No, this is one of the nice ones."

I remember one other interaction in that meeting. Mr. Glass told me how much he valued the education he had received at Missouri State and how he felt it had prepared him very well for his life's work. And then he said that I would be surprised by how many other people were like him—folks who had risen to the top of the business world after attending a local college or regional university that did not command much national recognition or prestige, but that had provided them an outstanding education. That observation got my attention, and over the next several years, I made something of a hobby out of collecting a list of the nationally prominent leaders who graduated from nonelite colleges.

Included on that list was Lee Scott, David Glass's successor as Walmart CEO, who graduated from Pittsburg State University in Kansas. Other notables were Howard Schultz, Starbuck's CEO and a graduate of Northern

Michigan University; Robert Nordelli, an alum of Western Illinois University, who became CEO of Chrysler; George Paz, a graduate of the University of Missouri, St. Louis, who served as the CEO of Express Scripts; Julian Goodman, former president of NBC and a graduate of Western Kentucky University; and David Bernauer, who was CEO of Walgreens from 2002 to 2006 and a graduate of North Dakota State University. The list also included several well-known public sector leaders, such as John Shalikashvili, a graduate of Bradley University, who went on to become the chair of the Joint Chiefs of Staff; Eastern Illinois University alum Jim Edgar, who was elected governor of Illinois; and John Cribbet, who graduated from Illinois Wesleyan and went on to become the chancellor of the University of Illinois.

Many years later this interest in influential people who were educated at some of the nation's lesser-known institutions was piqued again when I was serving as senior policy advisor to Missouri governor Jay Nixon. As I traveled with the governor and had the chance to meet other governors, I discovered that many of them also personified the theme first encountered years before—highly successful leaders who often attended accessible, affordable colleges that enjoyed little or no national prestige but that were credited by these men and women with changing their lives through transformative educational experiences.

Repeatedly, I heard stories about how a college education—often pursued at one of the in-state institutions of these governors-to-be—was the difference maker in their careers. They did not usually speak about the leading brand-name schools, the ones known for their high rejection rates or their endowments that ran to billions of dollars. Instead, they talked about the personal experiences at college that mattered the most to them. The faculty member with high standards who pushed them to excel. The coach who went beyond teaching them the Xs and Os of the game and focused on how to cope with the difficulties of life. The first campus election that they campaigned for. The internship that gave them that first glimpse of the work they wanted to do. The mentors who guided them through the various thickets of college life.

These stories made it clear that the impact of a college education was transmitted primarily through the personal relationships and practical experiences that future leaders participated in regardless of where they went to school. It did not depend on an institution's prestige, its national ranking, or its selectivity; rather, it depended on the meaningful, deep engagements that students were able to pursue at their institutions, and in many cases continue after they graduated.

After listening to several of these accounts I decided it was time to convert my on-again, off-again hobby into a systematic study of how American CEOs were educated, and so I began *Degrees and Pedigrees*. It is my attempt to describe the educational background—the "what, where, and how" of college—for a large sample of America's leading chief executives.

I wanted to write a book that answered several questions about CEO education: Where were our top executives educated, what did they study, how often did they go to graduate or professional school, did they usually attend elite colleges and universities, and what educational experiences did they say were most important for their careers?

My method was simple and straightforward. I examined the individual educational histories of 344 of the country's highest-profile chief executive officers, men and women who lead many of the largest and most influential organizations in America. While the details of their histories, both individually and cumulatively, reveal a great deal about the relative impact of various educational experiences on executive success, the stories themselves are often inspiring. They establish, repeatedly, the power and the promise of education, the process of what the poet Yeats called the "lighting of the fire." It is my hope that these histories help the reader gain a greater appreciation for the diversity of executive education in this country as well as for the components of that education that matter the most.

Acknowledgments

Several people helped me research and write this book, and I want to thank them for their sharp eyes, patient advice, and good judgment. Each one is an intelligent reader who caught the mistakes, improved the phrase, made the creative connections, and knew how to encourage a periodically discouraged author. Their many contributions resulted in this book's becoming much better than it would have been without them, and I owe them all my deepest gratitude. My thanks to Jay Nixon, Zora Mulligan, Christy Bertelson, and Mark Stringer for their many invaluable leads, comments, and edits to early drafts of the manuscript. I am grateful to Kelly McDonald for her invaluable assistance, most notably her remarkable success in teaching me the heretofore elusive ability to use the endnotes and table functions in Microsoft Word.

And finally, a particular and heartfelt thank-you is owed to my friend and colleague Paul Kincaid, who read and critiqued every version of every chapter, typically within just a few hours of the latest draft showing up in his email. He provoked many valuable improvements, serving in the delicate but crucial role of the friendly critic.

Chapter 1

Prestigious Colleges and Power Executives

Where are America's top executives educated? What do they study? Do they typically attend the nation's most elite colleges? Or do they, like millions of other students, choose colleges because of reasons like proximity, cost, and state pride? How important are graduate and professional degrees to their success? Is the MBA a prerequisite for becoming a CEO, or has it become an overvalued credential, whose bubble is about to burst?

These are the questions addressed in this book, based on a study of 344 of the country's highest-profile CEOs. Selected to represent a wide range of organizations and businesses, these individuals are the leaders of our largest businesses, local and state governments, armed services, private foundations, major media companies, and most prestigious universities and colleges. They are business titans, well-known to the public, the biggest of the big wheels.

The higher education backgrounds of these 344 individuals are examined in more detail in the ensuing chapters, with a special focus on those features that distinguish the different CEO groups from one another as well as the educational characteristics that tend to typify these backgrounds. But first, in this chapter, the topic of college rankings is examined—who does them, how they are conducted, which schools they tend to favor, and what the research says about the validity of such rating systems.

Following this brief review, a description of this sample of leading CEOs is provided, and the scope and influence of the enterprises they lead are highlighted. This is an impressive group, whose organizations affect the lives of all Americans every day. Examining where and how they were educated reveals a lot about how our leading executives are prepared, and it calls into question several assumptions about the role of elite colleges in this preparation.

THE COLLEGE RATINGS GAME

With every fall comes the unfolding of two American educational rituals. First, tens of thousands of ambitious high school juniors and seniors, usually with the assistance and insistence of their apprehensive parents, begin to scour the latest ratings and rankings of the nation's colleges and universities. At countless bookstores, newsstands, and websites, they pore over publications with titles such as "America's Top Colleges," "50 Colleges with the Best Professors," "Oxford Tops World University Rankings," and "The 50 Best Colleges in the U.S."

These ratings attract a rapt readership from many quarters—students, families, and the high school guidance counselors who advise them about college. Not surprisingly, the number of organizations churning out annual college rankings and ratings is growing.

Leading the list in longevity, readership, and influence is the *U.S. News and World Report*'s *Best Colleges*. First published in 1983, but revised and revamped several times over the years since, the *U.S. News* rating methodology relies on a formula that combines several measures of institutional functioning: student selectivity, retention and graduation rates, alumni donations, faculty resources, educational expenditures per student, and most controversially, a school's overall reputation as judged by peers.

Forbes, *Money*, *The Economist*, *The Princeton Review*, *Kiplinger's Best College Values*, *Washington Monthly*, *The Fiske Guide to Colleges*, and *College Prowler* also publish their own lists, each with different methodologies underlying the ratings/rankings. And various web-based ratings appear with increasing frequency, promoted like an academic Angie's List.

Published ratings are trusted by much of the American public to single out those institutions that will give students the highest-quality education. The top-ranked schools are further assumed to offer the strongest preparation for good jobs, the shortest odds for ultimate economic success, and the best-paved path to personal fulfillment. They become the *sine qua non*, the *summum bonum* of the college quest. As students begin the months-long process of deciding which college to attend, they and their families are often driven to the point of near desperation with gaining admission to at least one institution that, according to the ratings, stands out as one of America's premier colleges.

Having a son or daughter accepted at one of the designated elite schools becomes the holy grail for many families who have bought into the notion that their children's later success in life will all but be guaranteed by graduating from a "top-tier" college. And by implication, failure to make it into an elite institution is viewed with disappointment, if not dread. Attending a "second-tier" institution is feared as a failure predestining a "second-rate" education, and consequently, a "second-rate" career.

So it should come as no surprise that American families spend millions of dollars on expensive tutors, admissions coaches, ghostwriters of the required "personal" essays, SAT/ACT practice tests, and specialty summer camps, all aimed at boosting their children's chances for admission to at least one of the schools on the elite list. Often, this preparation is the culmination of years of strategically planned and doggedly determined grooming that begins as early as the search for just the right private preschool that will sharpen a toddler's competitive edge for college admission fifteen years later.

The burdens that families are willing to shoulder in this pursuit stretch far into the years after their children's college graduation. If necessary, Mom and Dad will take on the long-term obligation of significant personal debt to finance their child's attendance at one of America's highly esteemed, and very expensive, colleges.

The second ritual is closely linked to the first. It unfolds in the offices of university administrators across the country. They, too, are captivated by the latest college ratings. They study them in earnest because, like the applicants, the stakes with these ratings are also high for the administrators.

Will their institutions remain near the top of the ratings, move up the charts, or languish near the bottom? Climbing up a rung will likely translate into a surge in applications; slipping down a peg may lead to a dip in student interest. The ratings can also push up or pull down an institution's "yield" (the percentage of accepted students who subsequently enroll).

Administrators are privately ambivalent about this autumnal ritual. On the one hand, most of them know that college ratings, purporting to designate the "best" institutions, are highly flawed, and some university leaders have roundly condemned them. Among the strongest criticisms:

- Quality of education is very hard to measure, and no one, two, or eight proxies is adequate to the task.
- Reputational ratings, which play a prominent role in the *U.S. News* system, are notoriously subjective and inevitably self-fulfilling. They reward established institutions and shortchange newer ones that are making meaningful, but not yet well-recognized, changes.
- Selectivity—the percentage of applicants that an institution accepts—is easily manipulated by institutions, but it remains a factor in several of the rating schemes, nonetheless.
- Perceived quality of faculty is overdetermined by resources. Consequently, richer private schools will almost always fare better, regardless of whether their faculty are superior teachers or their graduates actually learn more than students from other institutions.

Any college administrator worth his or her salt can recite these objections plus ample others as to why the "Best Colleges in America" rankings don't—and shouldn't—mean as much as they do. And when administrators examine the latest ratings and discover that their institutions are ranked in one of the lower tiers, they will be quick to point out these flaws in defense of their own schools and as a justification for why they should be rated higher.

To be fair, some of the leaders of universities that score well are also highly critical of the ratings rat race and have even flat out refused to participate. In 2007, the presidents of more than fifty largely liberal arts colleges wrote a letter urging a boycott of the *U.S. News* survey. Known as the "Annapolis Letter," its signatories beseeched their colleagues "to refuse to use the rankings in any promotional efforts on behalf of your college or university, and more generally, refuse to refer to the rankings as an indication of the quality of your college or university."[1] And over the years, a few colleges—Reed, St. John's, and Lafayette are examples—have taken a firm stand and declined to participate in the annual *U.S. News* survey.

But then there is the other side of the coin. Most administrators not only participate in the ratings chase; they hasten, albeit perhaps with a guilty pleasure, to point out each and every rating that portrays their institution in the most favorable light, trying to persuade prospective students that it is the right place for them.

Go to any university's website and see if it doesn't cite whatever recent *Forbes*, *Money*, *Princeton Review*, or *U.S. News* rating it has received that puts it in the top ten for something—whether it is affordability, or value added, or student satisfaction, or social engagement. Colleges and universities aggressively market their product, and published ratings can be very useful—even if not reliable—validators of the qualities that an institution wants to claim.

Institutions often go to extraordinary lengths to boost their ratings, and it is no secret in academia that colleges have devised various strategies to "game" the ratings so they can improve their place in the standings.

Consider the variable of selectivity. The assumption by the designers of the rating systems is that the higher the percentage of applicants rejected for admission, the more selective and therefore the more elite an institution is. A college that accepts only 10 percent of its applicants must be more challenging and rigorous than one that admits twice that many.

It is easy for a university to pump up the number of applications it receives in any one year. In fact, admissions officials have publically admitted how they do so. Adding recruiter trips to targeted high schools, waiving the application fee, glossing up the campus brochures, luring more international applicants, and intensifying the social media contacts with student prospects are standard, and typically successful, strategies for drumming up more applications.

Of course, the additional applicants are unlikely to benefit from any better chances of admission. Instead, the college recruiters' come-on soon turns into the admission office's turndown. The result? The college can claim it has become more selective, thereby elevating its ranking. The baited applicants get only to feel the switch.

An extended critique of college rating systems is not the primary purpose of this book. Several other authors have documented the shortcomings of these ratings, and anyone interested in learning more about the foibles of the various schemes can consult such excellent works as:

- the 2015 book *Where You Go Is Not Who You'll Be* by Frank Bruni;[2]
- a 2011 *New Yorker* essay by Malcolm Gladwell[3] that drew unfavorable comparisons between the methods used by *U.S. News* and those employed by *Consumer Reports*; and
- a 2005 essay by Colin Driver, who at the time was president of Reed College, that explains why Reed stopped taking part in the ratings.[4]

The point that does need to be made is that tens of thousands of students and their families—to say nothing of the media and many members of the higher education establishment—take these ratings very seriously. They produce real and lasting consequences. Significant choices are made, alternative college plans are abandoned, family sacrifices are required, and large sums of money are invested—primarily because of the belief that graduating from a highly ranked college will eventually pay large and unique dividends.

HOW MUCH DOES COLLEGE PRESTIGE MATTER?

The evidence for a link between a college's reputation and the success of its graduates is mixed. Several studies show that graduating from an elite college results in numerous tangible benefits such as higher pay or quicker promotions. In general, the research shows that the earnings advantage of attending highly selective public universities or elite private schools ranges from 20 to 40 percent.

Other research qualifies this claim with several nuances. For example, a large-scale analysis of survey data by economists Eric Eide, Michael Hilmer, and Mark Showalter[5] showed that the earnings premium from attending a highly ranked school depends on the major and subsequent career of a student. They compared the earnings of 7,300 graduates ten years after they graduated from top-tier, middle-tier, or lower-tier schools, and they also looked at what majors these graduates had studied.

For business majors, the type of school mattered the most. Business graduates from top-tier schools were earning 12 percent more than business graduates from the middle-tier schools, who were making 6 percent more than their peers who attended a lower-tier school.

On the other hand, the prestige of a school mattered very little for engineering or science graduates. Social science and humanities majors also saw a salary bump from attending a more versus less prestigious school, but the gains were a little smaller than for the business graduates.

The *College Scorecard*

The largest source of data that addresses the relationship between college attended and income earned is the *College Scorecard*, a publicly available search engine launched by the US Department of Education at the direction of President Barack Obama. As highlighted in his 2013 State of the Union address, Obama intended the *Scorecard* to be a tool that "parents and students can use to compare schools based on a simple criteria [sic]: where you can get the most bang for your educational buck."

The *Scorecard* is a portal to several important measures such as the annual cost of attending an institution, the average debt for its students, and the college's graduation rate. It also reports students' median earned income, aggregated for the institutions they attended, ten years later. Although the Department of Education has avoided using these data to rank colleges, several other analysts have been less hesitant to examine these data to compare or rank order the performance of different institutions.

For example, consider the following ad-hoc comparison, using the 2017 college ratings compiled by *U.S. News and World Report.* Table 1.1 contains the median salary of students ten years after college for three groups of institutions:

- The top twenty national universities (all but one of which is a private school) contrasted with national universities ranked 81–100
- The top twenty public research universities versus the national universities ranked 81–100
- The top twenty national liberal arts colleges (of which eighteen are private) contrasted with liberal arts colleges ranked 61–80

At first glance, the results are dramatic. The median midcareer salary of students who attended a highly ranked national university was $72,100, significantly outpacing the earned income of students who went to a top twenty public research university ($54,400) or a top twenty national liberal arts college ($54,500).

Table 1.1 Median Salaries Ten Years after College by Type of Institution Attended

	National Universities	Public National Universities	National Liberal Arts Colleges
Top 20	$72,100	$54,400	$54,500
Middle-Tier	$49,900	$49,900	$48,600

Note: Middle-tier national and public national universities were those institutions ranked 81–100 among the 310 national universities ranked by the *U.S. News* in 2017. Middle-tier liberal arts colleges were ranked 61–80 among the 239 rankings in that category in the 2017 rankings.

Equally pronounced are the comparisons between the top universities in each category of institution with the lower-ranked schools in the same category. Students from a top twenty national university earned $22,200 more annually on average than those from a national university ranked 81–100. The annual income of students from a top twenty public university was $4,500 more than the average for those who attended a national university ranked 81–100, even though there are several private institutions in that cohort. And top twenty liberal arts alumni earned $5,900 a year more than students who attended a liberal arts college ranked 61–80.

But a closer look at the *Scorecard* methodology reveals just how complicated it can be to draw valid conclusions from these data. As it turns out, the results are far from definitive.

First, the figures for earned income are collected only for students who received federal financial aid while attending college. This approach introduces a serious confound. If institution A has a much higher percentage of students who receive aid compared to institution B, it becomes almost impossible to generalize about their respective impacts on alumni salaries. Since individuals' income tends to be correlated with the income of their family of origin, an institution with a higher percentage of federal loan recipients will be competing from a different starting point than one with a lower percentage of financially aided students.

Second, earned income is highly dependent on the occupations that students ultimately hold. It should come as no surprise that students from an institution that educates a high percentage of engineers (such as MIT or Georgia Tech) would have bigger salaries than students from a college without such a curriculum for the simple reason that engineers are paid more than teachers or social workers, regardless of the college they attended.

Research is clear on this point: if you are concerned about how much money you will make after college, your major matters. Anthony Carnevale, the director of the Center on Education and the Workforce at Georgetown University, is a leading authority who writes frequently about the links between education, career qualifications, and occupational outcomes. Carnevale and his colleagues Ban Cheah and Andrew Hanson analyzed the starting and midcareer salaries for 137 different undergraduate majors, sorted into groups like STEM (sciences, technology, engineering, mathematics), health, and the arts and humanities.[6]

They found that the entry-level salary of health majors was $41,000 annually; STEM majors earned $38,000; and arts and humanities students earned $29,000 on average. At midcareer, these salary differences grew even larger. STEM majors were earning an average of $76,000 annually, followed by health majors at $65,000, and arts and humanities graduates at $51,000.

The impact of a student's field of study is revealed in another study (*Ranking Your College: Where You Go and What You Make*) by Carnevale and his Georgetown colleagues.[7] Based on data from the 2015 *College Scorecard*, they tabulated the twenty colleges whose students earn the highest salaries ten years after starting their undergraduate studies. As you might expect, it includes powerhouses like Princeton, Stanford, the University of Pennsylvania, and Duke. But those brand-name schools are outnumbered by the likes of Harvey Mudd, Stevens Institute of Technology, the US Merchant Marine Academy, Bentley University, Kettering University, the SUNY Maritime College, Renesselaer Polytechnic Institute, and the Colorado School of Mines, all schools that do not top the ratings charts but that do specialize in preparing students for engineering, technology, or science-based industries.

Third, the *Scorecard* attributes a student's midcareer salary to any institution he or she attended, regardless of how long he or she was there. The income of students who graduated after four years of study at the same college is lumped in with those who attended an institution for only one semester. Likewise, if students from a given college go on to graduate school at another institution, their salaries will be larger as a result of their graduate education. However, with the *Scorecard*'s methodology, that salary advantage will be attributed entirely to the undergraduate school.

Finally, but perhaps most obviously, many of the qualities that help a student gain admission to a highly ranked school like Princeton or the University of California at Berkeley—factors like personal ambition and confidence, substantial family wealth, a lofty ACT or SAT score, a network of well-placed acquaintances—are the very same variables that correlate with later financial success, regardless of any added value that an outstanding school like Princeton might or might not have conveyed.

To tease apart these kinds of factors, Stacy Dale and Alan Krueger introduced a new variable into the usual study of the relationship between college prestige and graduates' earning power.[8] They looked at the colleges to which the students had applied in addition to the colleges they actually attended. This ingenious step allowed them to compare a student with a given SAT who, for example, had applied to Harvard but went to the University of Iowa with a student with the same SAT who attended Harvard.

When this variable was added, the link between attendance at elite schools and greater earnings by their graduates disappeared. As it turns out, given equivalent test scores, a student who applied to Harvard but attended Iowa instead earned on average the same as a student who actually attended Harvard. The average SAT score of the most selective school to which students apply ends up being a stronger predictor of their later earnings than the average SAT for the college where they eventually enroll. This remarkable finding did not hold up for all kinds of students, however. Minority students, low-income students, and students whose parents did not graduate from college all still reap a significant increase in later earnings after attending more elite colleges.

A 2017 study offers the most comprehensive study of the relationship between the income of students' families and the income that students themselves earned about ten years after leaving college. Stanford economist Raj Chetty led a team of researchers who conducted a massive analysis of all college students attending about 2,200 American colleges from 1999–2013.[9]

Based on federal student data and tax returns, the authors calculated every college's *mobility report card*, which was the percentage of its students who came from families in the bottom 20 percent of the income distribution and ended up in the upper 20 percent based on the income they earned in their early thirties. This mobility rate is computed as the product of the percentage of a college's enrolled students whose families were in the lowest income quintile times the percentage of those students with postcollege earnings that reached the top quintile.

As it turns out, the top ten mobility rates were all at nonelite public colleges, primarily because they were successful with the larger number of students from low-income backgrounds that they admit compared to elite schools. To be sure, elite schools are very successful in boosting low-income students to the top 20 percent based on their postcollege earnings, but because they admit relatively small numbers of these students, their overall upward mobility rates are lower.

The top ten upward mobility colleges were all located in New York, California, and Texas. In order, they were California State University (Los Angeles); Pace University; SUNY at Stony Brook; Technical Career Institutes (a two-year college in New York); University of Texas–Pan American, the City University of New York system; Glendale Community College; South Texas College; California State Polytechnic–Pomona; and the University of Texas at El Paso.

The picture changes dramatically, however, if we calculate the mobility rates as the fraction of students who jump from the lowest quintile of family income all the way to the top 1 percent based on their own income as they reach their thirties. This top ten list is dominated by elite colleges, all but one of which is private: the University of California (Berkeley), Columbia, MIT, Stanford, Swarthmore College, Johns Hopkins, New York University, the University of Pennsylvania, Cornell, and the University of Chicago.

One other encouraging finding from this study was that low- and high-income students who attend a given college fare about equally well in terms of their later earnings. For example, the gap in postcollege earnings between students who came from the highest- and lowest-income families was very small—only about 7 percent, confirming the belief that college can be an equalizer of opportunity by leveling the playing field for students from low-income backgrounds.

Payscale's "College Salary Report"

Payscale operates an interactive website, "The College Salary Report," that ranks colleges on the basis of the average early-career and midcareer salaries for their graduates. More than 1,000 undergraduate institutions are represented.

The 2016–2017 version of the "College Salary Report"[10] also reports the percentage of graduates with STEM degrees, given the salary premium of those majors. Its findings mirror those found by Carnevale. Counted among Payscale's top twenty institutions are a handful of elite colleges plus several engineering schools, and three federal service academies—the US Military Academy at West Point, the Naval Academy at Annapolis, and the Air Force Academy at Colorado Springs, each of which obviously conveys a distinct occupational advantage—indeed, a job requirement—on its graduates.

The *Gallup-Purdue Index*

In partnership with Purdue University and the Lumina Foundation, Gallup surveyed nearly 30,000 college alumni in 2014 about their perceptions of how their undergraduate education related to five measures of well-being after graduation. This was the first of an anticipated five annual surveys. In its initial report, Gallup found "no difference in workplace engagement or a college graduate's well-being if they attended a public or private not-for-profit institution, a highly selective institution, or a top 100 school."[11]

Gallup conducted a second survey in 2015. Like the first one, it did not measure graduates' salaries.[12] Instead, it focused on their personal assessments of well-being in five domains:

• Purpose—being motivated to achieve goals and liking what you do each day
• Social well-being—having strong relationships and love in your life

- Physical well-being—enjoying good health and having the energy to get things done
- Financial well-being—managing your economic life to reduce stress and feel secure
- Community well-being—liking where you live and having pride in your community

Frank Bruni asked the Gallup researchers to conduct a special follow-up analysis for him that compared three groups: the graduates of the top fifty national universities in the *U.S. News* rankings, the graduates of *U.S. News* top fifty liberal arts and colleges, and the overall sample of graduates in the Gallup survey. In *Where You Go Is Not Who You'll Be*, Bruni summarizes the results of this analysis:[13]

- Ten percent of all college graduates judged themselves to be thriving on all five of the surveyed dimensions compared to 11 percent of graduates from the top fifty national universities and 13 percent for graduates from the elite liberal arts schools.
- In terms of employment, 39 percent of all the graduates felt highly engaged and committed to their jobs. This figure nudged up to 41 percent for the top-ranked national university alumni and 47 percent for the elite-college graduates.

These contrasts, along with others that Bruni reports in his book, point to a consistent, but in most instances negligible, advantage for the most esteemed schools. Far more important for graduates' later well-being than the prestige of the school they attended was the personal experiences they crafted for themselves on campus. The results consistently pointed to the positive impact of students being deeply engaged in their institutions and their own education.

As summarized by Bruni, "thrivers" were much more likely to have had a professor in school who cared about them as a person, to have had trusted mentors who encouraged and pushed them toward their dreams, and to have worked at an internship or job where they could apply what they had learned in the classroom.

The key was not what colleges students attended, but whether they experienced meaningful, challenging relationships wherever they enrolled. The lasting impact of their college education depended much more on rich, extensive, personal engagements rather than on the exclusivity of the institution.

As we examine the education of America's leading executives in the ensuing chapters, the same conclusion will be driven home repeatedly: it's not so much where they went; it's what they did that proves to be more crucial. Graduating from an elite college gives an individual several advantages, but those advantages also can be created or approximated at many other kinds of institutions. Ultimately, for most of these leaders, it's the personal pursuits at college, rather than the proclaimed prestige of college, that matters more.

The Brookings Institution's "Value-Added" Ratings

Jonathan Rothwell, Fellow at the Brookings Institution, used Payscale and *College Scorecard* data to develop what he termed a "value-added" ranking of colleges.[14] A college's value added is calculated by comparing what its graduates earn after graduation with what they would be expected to earn based on (1) their entering personal characteristics (academic preparation, family income, a few demographic variables) and (2) several features of the colleges themselves (curricular offerings, the percentage of STEM graduates, student completion rates). In order, he reported that the top ten colleges, based on their alumni's average midcareer earnings, were:

- California Institution of Technology
- Colgate University
- Massachusetts Institute of Technology
- Rose-Hulman Institute of Technology
- Carleton College
- Washington and Lee University
- SUNY Maritime College
- Clarkson University
- Manhattan College
- Stanford University

This list includes only six schools (MIT, Washington and Lee, Colgate, Cal Tech, Carleton, and Stanford) from the three *U.S. News* top twenty ranking lists. More than student selectivity, size of the university endowment, or reputation of the faculty, high value-added colleges tended to be those that had a strong STEM orientation, offered generous financial aid, and graduated students on time.

POWER EXECUTIVES/PRESTIGIOUS COLLEGES

To take a fresh look at the relationship between career success and college education, individuals who had achieved the highest levels of executive leadership were first identified and then their educational histories were examined. The starting point was to identify a very select sample of individuals, people who had reached the pinnacle of executive leadership in their fields.

The focus was not to analyze a college degree's impact on these individuals' income. Rather, the intent was to study the educational histories of influential leaders, regardless of their salaries. No doubt the income of many of the executives who were studied would make them "one percenters," but many others—particularly the elected CEOs and military leaders—do not earn eye-popping salaries.

Rather than starting with an examination of the graduates of certain institutions and comparing their career outcomes with graduates from other colleges, the approach involved selecting elite individuals, leaders who had reached the peak positions in their fields, and then working back to explore their college experiences.

Using this method, it was possible to answer the two basic questions posed in this book: Where are America's leading executives educated, and what do they study?

From these two basic questions, several others immediately follow. Do top executives graduate from mostly highly prestigious institutions, or do their alma maters range across the educational spectrum? Are certain undergraduate majors or graduate degrees the predominant preparation for executive leadership, or is degree specialization not all that relevant? Which institutions lead the pack in educating America's top executives? Do high-level executives major in the humanities, or do they prefer more technical disciplines? Were they typically trained as scientists, economists, or lawyers? For what executive careers is a PhD necessary? How essential is the vaunted MBA?

To answer these questions, a sample of 344 of the nation's leading executives, chosen to represent various sectors of business and different types of institutions, was selected. Because the primary interest was the education of the very highest echelon of American executive leadership, the focus was placed on executives who were in charge of America's largest or most influential enterprises. And unlike prior studies that examined the education of only one kind of leader (governors, or Fortune 500 CEOs, or military leaders), this study concentrated on the education of major American executives, broadly construed.

This executive sample was drawn from a wide range of organizations—public and private, for profit and not for profit, governmental and nongovernmental—engaged in varied sectors of the economy. Leaders in seven domains, as of 2016, were identified, and their educational histories are analyzed in the next seven chapters:

- Chapter 2 focuses on 100 *publicly elected chief executives*—specifically, the nation's fifty governors and the mayors of America's fifty largest cities.
- In chapter 3, the education of fifty *private enterprise CEOs* is examined. The sample includes the leaders of the thirty companies in the Dow

Industrial Index plus the CEOs of the twenty largest Fortune 500 companies, not included in the Dow Index.

- Chapter 4 considers the world of *philanthropy*. The education of the CEOs of the fifty largest foundations in the United States is reviewed.
- In chapter 5, attention shifts to the *military*, with an inspection of the educational profiles of the forty active-duty, four-star officers in the uniformed services of the United States (thirteen in the Air Force, eleven in the Army, ten in the Navy, four in the Marines, and two in the Coast Guard).
- Chapter 6 is concerned with the *news media* and the education of the publishers of the forty US newspapers with the largest daily circulation (because two people split the publisher duties at one newspaper, the final number of publishers was forty-one) plus the CEOs of the ten leading TV news channels in the country.
- *Higher education* is the topic of chapter 7. Where did the leaders of our most prestigious colleges and universities go to school? The histories of the presidents and chancellors of the twenty top-ranked national universities, the twenty top national public universities, and the ten mostly highly ranked liberal arts colleges are considered. Because of ties in some of the rankings, there were fifty-three presidents/chancellors included in this grouping.
- Finally, in chapter 8, the degrees and pedigrees of all 344 individuals are tabulated, and the implications of the collective outcomes are discussed.

The economic and social impact of the organizations led by these individuals is staggering. Collectively, they generate trillions of dollars of revenue. These CEOs administer budgets that annually top a trillion dollars in expenditures of taxpayer money. They employ tens of millions of workers, educate millions of students, and exert some sort of daily influence on the lives of virtually every American.

To gain a slightly better appreciation of the magnitude of these entities, consider the following indicators:

- The combined market capitalization of the Dow 30 in 2016 was $5.4 trillion, which is more than the GDP of all the countries in the world, except the United States and China. The pooled 2015 revenue of these companies was $2.7 trillion, which was not even their high water mark, having suffered a small decline from the four prior years.
- In FY 2016, the fifty states spent just shy of $800 billion in general revenue and employed over five million workers.
- More than forty-eight million people—15 percent of all Americans—live in our fifty largest cities. The mayors of these cities were responsible for combined municipal budgets that exceeded $185 billion.

- The total print circulation of the forty largest newspapers in the United States accounts for roughly 40 percent of the forty million newspapers that were circulated daily in the United States in 2016. When it comes to news, about two-thirds of Americans watch at least one of the major network news shows on a regular basis, and more than a third of Americans watch the news on one of the cable news shows.
- The combined assets of the country's fifty largest foundations exceed $250 billion. In 2014 alone, these foundations doled out more than $15 billion in grants and gifts.
- More than two million people serve in active-duty or reserve status in the armed forces of the United States, and the United States spent about $580 billion to fund these forces in 2016.
- More than 800,000 undergraduate students are being educated at the fifty-three colleges and universities included in this sample. Add in graduate and professional studies, and their total enrollment exceeds one million students.

Having drawn this sample of leading executives, there was one additional task to complete. Because one of the questions to answer was whether there was indeed a link between college prestige and CEO stardom, a definition of what constituted an elite or prestigious institution was needed.

The following method was used to identify fifty "top-ranked" institutions: based on the 2017 *U.S. News* rankings of national universities, public national universities, and national liberal arts colleges, the top twenty institutions in the first two categories and the top ten institutions in the national liberal arts category were selected.

Because of ties, fifty-three institutions ended up in the top fifty. They are listed in table 1.2. Throughout the rest of the book when reference is made to "top-ranked" institutions, these are the schools that are included.

This approach is admittedly problematic because it carries a risk for unintended consequences. Above all, it is important to avoid perpetuating the myth that the top-ranked schools occupy some hallowed category of superiority, that they are the only institutions that can deliver an inspiring, life-changing education. American higher education is envied worldwide in large measure because of the diversity of institutions at which students can choose to be educated. It is a mistake to view it as a caste system, topped by a list of Brahmin-like schools.

Examining this aspect of the connection between CEO achievement and educational background allowed the exploration of one question of particular interest—whether there is, in fact, any relationship, and if so, how large—between graduating from a top-ranked college as conventionally defined by the rating systems and ascending to the highest ranks of American executive leadership. To address this issue required employing some classification

Table 1.2   Top-Ranked American Universities and Colleges

National Universities	Public National Universities	National Liberal Arts Colleges
Princeton	U. California (Berkeley)	Williams College
Harvard	UCLA	Amherst College
U. Chicago	U. Virginia	Wellesley College
Yale	U. Michigan	Middlebury College
Columbia	U. North Carolina	Swarthmore College
Stanford	William & Mary	Bowdoin College
MIT	Georgia Institute of Technology	Carleton College
Duke	U. California (Santa Barbara)	Pomona College
U. Pennsylvania	U. California (Irvine)	Claremont McKenna College
Johns Hopkins	U. California (Davis)	Davidson College
Dartmouth	U. California (San Diego)	
California Institute of Technology	U. Illinois	
Northwestern	U. Wisconsin	
Brown	Pennsylvania State U.	
Cornell	U. Florida	
Rice	Ohio State U.	
Notre Dame	U. Washington	
Vanderbilt	U. Georgia	
Washington U.	U. Texas	
Emory	Purdue U.	
Georgetown	U. Connecticut	
	U. Maryland	

Note: The University of California (Berkeley) was tied for twentieth among the national universities and was ranked first among the public national universities. It is listed only once, in the public national universities category.

of exalted institutions, regardless of whether such exaltation is ultimately viewed as more fable than fact. Given the purposes of the book, it is best to recognize that the specification of a list of "top-ranked" schools was a methodological requirement, not an objective assessment of quality.

NOTES

1. http://www.educationconservancy.org/presidents_letter.html
2. Frank Bruni, *Where You Go Is Not Who You'll Be: An Antidote to College Admissions Mania* (New York: Grand Central Publishing, 2015).
3. Malcolm Gladwell, "The order of things: What college ratings really tell us." *The New Yorker*, Feb. 14 & 21, 2011.
4. Colin Driver, "Is there life after rankings?" *The Atlantic*, November 2005.
5. Eric R. Eide, Michael J. Hilmer, and Mark H. Showalter, "Is it where you go or what you study? The relative influence of college selectivity and college

major on earnings," *Contemporary Economic Policy 34* (2016): 37–46, doi: 10.111/coep.12115.

6. Anthony Carnevale, Ban Cheah, and Andrew Hanson, *The Economic Value of College Majors* (Washington, DC: Georgetown University Center on Education and the Workforce, 2015).

7. Anthony Carnevale, Ban Cheah, and Martin Van Der Werf, *Ranking Your College: Where You Go and What You Make* (Washington, DC: Georgetown University Center on Education and the Workforce, 2015). https://cew.georgetown.edu/wp-content/uploads/College-Scorecard-Web.pdf

8. Stacey Dale and Alan Krueger, *Estimating the Payoff to Attending a More Selective College: An Application of Selection on Observables and Unobservables*, National Bureau of Economic Research No. 7322 (August 1999).

9. http://www.equality-of-opportunity.org/papers/coll_mrc_paper.pdf

10. https://www.payscale.com/college-salary-report

11. http://www.purdue.edu/newsroom/releases/2014/Q2/gallup-purdue-index-releases-inaugural-findings-of-national-landmark-study.html

12. http://www.purdue.edu/newsroom/gallup/docs/GPI_overview.pdf

13. Bruni, *Where You Go Is Not Who You'll Be.*

14. https://www.brookings.edu/research/beyond-college-rankings-a-value-added-approach-to-assessing-two-and-four-year-schools/

Chapter 2

Elected CEOs

In the fall of 1970, soon after arriving on campus at Ohio State University, a brash, working-class freshman had become fed up with conditions in the high-rise dormitory to which he had been assigned. Chief among his gripes was a rule against residents opening the windows in their dorm rooms. He thought that was a stupid prohibition, and he wanted the university to get rid of it. After repeatedly getting a deaf ear from campus housing officials, he decided to take his complaints to the top. He began to badger the university president's office to give him an appointment so he could present his case.

Eventually, he wore the administrative staff down and secured an appointment with OSU president Novice Fawcett. In that meeting, after lodging his objections about the dorm windows, the young freshman took full advantage of his time with Fawcett and proceeded to ask him exactly what it was a university president does. Fawcett recited the usual list—strategic planning, academic oversight, personnel decisions, fundraising—and then happened to mention that the next day he was going to Washington, DC, to meet with President Richard M. Nixon.

Without missing a beat, the young student said that there were some things he himself would like to talk to Nixon about and wondered if he could go along with Fawcett. Wisely, Fawcett declined to drag him along. But the freshman didn't take no as the final answer. He asked Fawcett if he would at least be willing to deliver a letter to Nixon for him. Whether bemused or exasperated, Fawcett agreed.

The student wrote the letter—on his personal stationery, in long hand. In it, he praised Nixon "not only as a great president but an even greater person." He continued: "Would it be possible for me to come to the White House to talk and see you sometime in the future? I would immediately pass up a Rose Bowl trip to see you. My parents would permit me to fly down anytime, and I know my grades wouldn't suffer." Predicting a Nixon election victory in 1972, the student implored the president: "this is probably a ridiculous request but to me it would be a dream come true."[1]

True to his word, Fawcett delivered the letter. In a matter of days, Nixon responded with a letter of his own. He wrote: "I would be happy to have the opportunity to welcome you to the White House at some time in the not too distant future, and I have asked that someone on my staff get in touch with you to make the various arrangements necessary."[2]

Official White House logs show that on December 22, 1970, Nixon made phone calls to Senator Barry Goldwater and Secretary of State William Rogers. He held some staff meetings and signed a bill into law. The logs also confirm that he met with a freshman from Ohio State University from 12:31 to 12:51 p.m. Originally promised five minutes of the president's time, the freshman was not to be shortchanged. As he later recalled, "They were going to have to yank me out of this place, because I wasn't leaving after five minutes."[3]

Nixon's next meeting started late. Henry Kissinger had to wait until President Nixon finished up talking with that gutsy Ohio State freshman. The student's name? John Kasich. The same John Kasich who went on to become a member of Congress, chair of the House Budget Committee, the two-time governor of Ohio, and in 2016, a Republican contender himself for president of the United States.

John Kasich's story may be unusual in its details. Not many college freshmen elbow their way into the college president's office, let alone successfully solicit their own personal invitation from the president of the United States to meet in the White House. But the Kasich incident is important because it sheds light on the main questions posed in this book.

What are the distinctive qualities in the higher education background of America's top executives, like our governors and big-city mayors? What features of their education were most instrumental to their careers? Were they typically products of the country's elite, highly selective institutions, or did they tend to graduate from more accessible colleges? What were their college majors? Did they go on to graduate and professional study, and if so, what was the nature of that advanced work?

As we will discover, John Kasich's college history illustrates some of the educational features we find with governors and many high-profile executives in other fields. While almost all of them are college graduates and many have graduate degrees, the majority of them did not graduate from one of America's top-ranked institutions. Many did go to one of the Ivy League schools or other top-tier colleges, and they no doubt received outstanding educations at them. But more striking is the number of executive superstars who started their education at a community college or those who stayed close to home and attended their state university or a small liberal arts college.

Religiously affiliated colleges, urban universities, and the service academies also figure prominently in the background of these executives. Graduating from a prestigious university conveys real advantages to those who aspire
to the pinnacles of leadership, but it is by no means the only path to such
success. The careers of our country's top elected executives—the nation's
governors and the mayors of our fifty largest cities—illustrate this pattern
very well.

GOVERNORS

All fifty of the governors serving in office in 2016 attended college, and forty-
eight completed at least an undergraduate degree. Gary Herbert (Utah) enrolled
at Brigham Young University but did not earn a degree, and Scott Walker
(Wisconsin) attended Marquette University but did not complete his studies.

The fifty governors earned a total of eighty-seven undergraduate, graduate,
and professional degrees. These degrees are listed in table 2.1.

Overall, more than half of the governors' degrees were awarded by private
institutions. This is mildly surprising. Governors are probably the leading
example of a public CEO, and yet they tended—by a small but noteworthy
margin—to earn their degrees from private colleges and universities.

No one institution stands out as a uniquely fertile educational cradle for
future governors. Only nine schools awarded degrees to more than one governor. Of the nine, four were Ivy League schools. Yale led the pack with four,
followed by Harvard with three. Each of the following institutions granted
degrees to two different governors: Brown, Dartmouth, Wesleyan, Lewis
and Clark, Ohio State, Northwestern, and University of Chicago. Other than
the four Ivy League schools, there really is not much of an institutional concentration. The eighty-seven undergraduate and graduate degrees earned by
governors were awarded by sixty-five different institutions.

Undergraduate Study

With respect to the undergraduate institutions that the governors attended,
twenty-seven were private and twenty-three were public. Five universities
graduated two governors apiece—Brown, Dartmouth, Harvard, Yale, and
Wesleyan University. Add to this list such top-ranked public universities
as University of California at Berkeley, University of Michigan, Ohio State
University, University of Texas, and University of Washington, along with
leading private institutions such as Emory University, Claremont McKenna,
and University of Chicago, and you have an impressive group of highly
ranked schools.

Table 2.1 Governors' Education

State	Governor	Undergraduate Degree	Graduate Degree
Alabama	Robert J. Bentley	BS Biology/Chemistry University of Alabama	MD U. Alabama
Alaska	Bill Walker	BS Business Management Lewis & Clark College	JD U. Puget Sound
Arizona	Douglas A. Ducey	BS Finance Arizona State U.	
Arkansas	William Asa Hutchinson	BS Accounting Bob Jones U.	JD U. Arkansas
California	Edmund G. Brown	BA Classics U. California (Berkeley)	JD Yale
Colorado	John W. Hickenlooper	BA English Wesleyan U.	MS Geology Wesleyan U.
Connecticut	Dannel P. Malloy	BA Political Science/Sociology Boston College	JD Boston College
Delaware	Jack A. Markell	BA Economics/Developmental Studies Brown	MBA U. Chicago
Florida	Richard L. Scott	BA Business Admin. U. Missouri (Kansas City)	JD Southern Methodist U.
Georgia	John Nathan Deal	BA Mercer U.	JD Mercer U.
Hawaii	David Y. Ige	BS Electrical Engineering U. Hawaii (Manoa)	MBA/Decision Science U. Hawaii (Manoa)
Idaho	Clement L. "Butch" Otter	BA Political Science College of Idaho	
Illinois	Bruce V. Rauner	BA Economics Dartmouth	MBA Harvard
Indiana	Michael R. Pence	BA History Hanover College	JD Indiana U.
Iowa	Terry E. Branstad	BA Political Science U. Iowa	JD Drake U.
Kansas	Samuel D. Brownback	BS Ag Economics Kansas State U.	JD U. Kansas
Kentucky	Matthew G. Bevin	BA Eastern Asian Studies Washington and Lee U.	
Louisiana	John B. Edwards	BS Engineering US Military Academy	JD Louisiana State U.
Maine	Paul R. LePage	BS Business Admin. Husson U.	MBA U. Maine (Orono)
Maryland	Lawrence J. Hogan Jr.	BA Government/Political Science Florida State U.	
Massachusetts	Charles D. Baker Jr.	BA English Harvard	MBA Northwestern
Michigan	Richard D. Snyder	BA General Studies U. Michigan	MBA and JD U. Michigan
Minnesota	Mark B. Dayton	BA Psychology Yale	
Mississippi	Dewey "Phil" Bryant	BA Criminal Justice U. Southern Mississippi	MA Political Science Mississippi College
Missouri	Jeremiah "Jay" Nixon	BA Political Science U. Missouri	JD U. Missouri
Montana	Stephen C. Bullock	BA Philosophy/Politics/Economics Claremont McKenna College	JD Columbia
Nebraska	John "Pete" Ricketts	BA Biology U. Chicago	MBA U. Chicago

State	Name	Undergraduate	Graduate
Nevada	Brian E. Sandoval	BA English U. Nevada	JD Ohio State U.
New Hampshire	Margaret Hassan	BA History Brown	JD Northeastern U.
New Jersey	Christopher J. Christie	BA Political Science U. Delaware	JD Seton Hall U.
New Mexico	Susana A. Martinez	BA Criminal Justice U. Texas (El Paso)	JD U. Oklahoma
New York	Andrew M. Cuomo	BA Fordham U.	JD U. Albany
North Carolina	Patrick L. McCrory	BS Political Science/Education Catawba College	
North Dakota	John S. "Jack" Dalrymple	BA American Studies Yale	
Ohio	John R. Kasich	BA Political Science Ohio State U.	
Oklahoma	Mary Fallin	BS Human and Environmental Studies Oklahoma State U.	
Oregon	Katherine Brown	BA Environmental Conservation U. Colorado	JD Lewis & Clark College
Pennsylvania	Thomas W. Wolf	BA Government Dartmouth	MPhil Philosophy U. London PhD Political Science MIT
Rhode Island	Gina M. Raimondo	BA Economics Harvard	DPhil – Sociology Oxford JD Yale
South Carolina	Nikki Haley	BS Accounting Clemson U.	JD Northwestern U.
South Dakota	Dennis M. Daugaard	BS Government U. South Dakota	
Tennessee	William E. Haslam	BA History Emory U.	JD Vanderbilt U.
Texas	Gregory W. Abbott	BA Finance U. Texas	
Utah	Gary R. Herbert	Attended Brigham Young U.	
Vermont	Peter E. Shumlin	BA English/Government Studies Wesleyan U.	
Virginia	Terence R. McAuliffe	BA Political Science Catholic U.	JD Georgetown U.
Washington	Jay R. Inslee	BA Economics U. Washington	JD Willamette U.
West Virginia	Earl R. Tomlin	BS Business Management West Virginia U.	MBA Marshall U.
Wisconsin	Scott K. Walker	Attended Marquette U.	
Wyoming	Matthew H. Mead	BA Radio/Television Trinity U.	JD U. Wyoming

This pattern illustrates the difficulty in drawing any overly broad conclusions about the educational backgrounds of high-level executives. The "top-ranked" schools provided an undergraduate education to about a third of the nation's governors in office during 2016, but approximately two-thirds of the governors received their undergraduate degrees from colleges that do not rank in the *U.S. News* 2017 lists of top twenty private universities, top twenty public universities, or top ten liberal arts colleges. Is this glass a third full or two-thirds empty?

Gubernatorial alma maters span a wide range of governance, size, and mission. Included on the governors' resumes are major public research universities (Arizona State University, Clemson University, University of Iowa, and University of Missouri, for example), private liberal arts colleges (Hanover and Husson), religiously affiliated schools (Bob Jones University and Catawba College), urban campuses (University of Missouri at Kansas City and Fordham), and the US Military Academy.

Adding to this diversity are community colleges, which have a long and admirable track record as institutions that promote access to higher education. First-generation college students often start their postsecondary education at a community college, as do many students from low-income backgrounds. The nation's community colleges also have done an outstanding job of welcoming and educating adults returning to college. But community colleges have served would-be governors as well:

- The son of an electrician, Idaho governor Bruce Otter lived in a number of small towns across the West and Midwest throughout his youth. He attended fifteen different elementary and secondary schools and worked several odd jobs in high school to help support himself and his family. Otter attended Boise Junior College before earning his BA in political science from the College of Idaho in Caldwell, Idaho, becoming the first member of his family to graduate from college.
- Phil Bryant, the governor of Mississippi, earned an associate's degree in criminal justice from Hinds Community College, just down the road from Jackson, Mississippi, where Bryant would eventually reside in the governor's mansion.
- At the age of sixteen, while still attending Lakeview High School, Rick Snyder took a business class from nearby Kellogg Community College. He went on to take more classes from Kellogg at night and on the weekends. By the time he graduated from high school several months early to enroll at the University of Michigan, Snyder had accumulated twenty-five college credits. In 2014, Kellogg conferred an associate of arts degree to Rick Snyder. "Dual enrollment was a wonderful opportunity for me and my family," he said about what has become a very popular strategy among today's high

school students who are attempting to hold down the costs of a college education. Governor Snyder continued: "I wouldn't be who I am today but for Kellogg Community College. I'm proud to say I am an alumni now."[4]

Just over half of the governors (twenty-six) pursued their undergraduate studies at an institution that is located in the state that elected them to office. This is a pattern worth attention. What is it about attending an in-state college that is advantageous to an aspiring state leader? Maybe, it's simply a matter of state pride and loyalty, or perhaps it is because it affords leadership opportunities outside the classroom that the public begins to notice, allowing would-be candidates to build name recognition. Gaining a position of campus leadership can help launch a career because it gives the student a chance to establish initial home-turf notoriety.

Several governors began to hone their political skills on a college campus, and what better place to do so than a school in the state you would later govern. Georgia governor Nathan Deal was student body president at Mercer University, where he also was selected as the commander of the ROTC cadets. Although he was admitted to MIT, David Ige, the governor of Hawaii, turned down that offer and enrolled instead at the University of Hawaii, where he was chosen to be student body secretary. Doug Ducey was elected the president of Arizona State University's Inter Fraternity Council. In 2015, he was sworn in as the twenty-third governor of Arizona.

Other governors were successful college politicians, albeit at a school outside of their governed state. As examples, New Jersey's governor, Chris Christie, was elected student body president at the University of Delaware, and John Bel Edwards of Louisiana was elected by his classmates to be the vice chairman of the honor code panel at the US Military Academy at West Point.

After moving from Maryland to Florida following his parents' divorce, Maryland governor Larry Hogan attended Florida State University in the state capital of Tallahassee, in large part because at that time Florida offered free tuition to in-state students. While at Florida State, where he majored in government, Hogan worked for the house minority leader in the Florida House of Representatives. This allowed him to sharpen the political skills he had first learned at a very early age from his father, Lawrence Hogan Sr., a three-term congressman representing Maryland's Fifth Congressional District. Upon graduation, Hogan first worked on Capitol Hill for a California congressman, but he soon turned to Maryland politics again, helping his dad win the race for Prince George county executive and then working for him as a liaison.

Not every governor's college political career has been auspicious. Even though he never graduated from Marquette, Scott Walker ran for student body president but lost in a hotly contested campus election. Despite being active in the student government association, Pat McCrory lost twice in his bid to be the student body president of Catawba College, a small, religiously affiliated, liberal arts college in Salisbury, North Carolina. He went on to be a seven-term mayor of Charlotte, and in 2012, was elected governor of North Carolina, the first Republican governor in that state in twenty years.

In general, however, attending an in-state school has proven to be a distinct advantage for future governors. It gave them the experience of becoming public leaders, if even on a small scale. They had the chance to appear in front of audiences, debate opponents, and craft a persuasive message and defend it against criticism. And perhaps even more importantly, it enabled them to begin to build the networks of friends and confidants who would come to serve them well in later campaigns and their administrations.

Interviewed about his educational background, Jay Nixon, the two-term governor of Missouri said, "there is no better connection for a politician in Missouri than the University of Missouri Law School. The graduates from there eventually touch every county, every courthouse in the state. And you are jammed together with hundreds of them for three years. You can really build a core of strength around the friends you make and keep from law school."

After graduating from high school, Nixon made a beeline to the University of Missouri. A native of Desoto, a small town southwest of St. Louis, he said that the University of Missouri (or MU as the campus in Columbia is known) was the only school to which he applied. His mother and father both went there, and he really never gave any other college much thought. In fact, his mother returned to MU later in life to earn her PhD and was on campus at the same time her son was an undergraduate, a feature of campus life that Nixon admitted made him occasionally uneasy: "not many guys dream of going to college with their mother."

Politics was in Nixon's blood. His mother was the president of the local school board. His father served as mayor of Desoto. Nixon recalls that his Eagle Scout project at age thirteen consisted of asking his fellow students that if given the chance what questions would they like to ask the school board president, the mayor, and the chief of police. He bundled these questions together and then talked a local radio station into broadcasting three separate programs with him interviewing the local officials.

When it came to choosing an undergraduate major at MU, it was no surprise that Nixon chose political science. It was a good preparation for law school, and by then Nixon had decided he wanted to be a lawyer, like his father.

Political science also required the smallest number of credits within a major, allowing Nixon to take a larger number of electives than would have been the case in other majors. He felt at the time that he was not as well read as he should be, so he took every Shakespeare class that was available. "I took the hardest courses I could. I would read those plays and listen to them too. William Jones (the professor of the classes on Shakespeare) was one of the faculty members I admired the most at Mizzou, and I still take a lot of pride in doing well in his classes."

MU also afforded Nixon a chance to try his hand at campus politics. Like many others who ultimately became governors, he served in student government as a senator. But it was two other positions that gave him an opportunity to learn how elected officials build and exert influence on behalf of a constituency.

Nixon served a term as the chief justice of the student traffic appeals court. This court had a weekly docket, and Nixon, along with his fellow judges, had the power to enforce or forgive the on-campus traffic tickets that the MU students appealed. It was a position with the responsibility to make real-world decisions and dole out the ensuing consequences, and while its subject matter may seem trivial now, it allowed Nixon to learn some early, important lessons about public persuasion and decision making.

The second campus position at MU was even closer to Nixon's heart. An avid basketball player who spent every day playing pickup games at the Rothwell-Brewer gym, Nixon maneuvered himself to be the student chair of the committee that set the rules about who had priority access to the gym.

Annoyed that the ROTC cadets were being given preference to use court space for their marching drills, Nixon arranged for the committee to relegate them to a field outside the gym so that he and his intramural teams could have more time on the courts. He recounts: "I really never got that much out of being a student senator, but being able to help students with their traffic tickets and win more court time for me and my teammates, those were big deals."

After graduation Nixon entered the law school at the University of Missouri. Once again, it was the only school to which he applied. In fact, he said that on the very first day that applications for admission were being accepted, "I hand-delivered my application to the Dean's office. I was determined to be in the first wave they considered. Why not? I knew exactly what I wanted to do and where I wanted to do it."

Nixon finished MU law school in 1981 and returned to Desoto to practice law in the firm where his father was a senior partner. But it was not too long before he launched his first formal political campaign for a state office. In 1986 he was elected state senator, representing the citizens of Jefferson County and beginning what would eventually become a thirty-year career in elected office, capped by his election to successive terms as governor in 2008 and 2012.

Nixon knew how to capitalize on his time at the state's flagship university. And we see that same advantage being turned by several other governors who followed up their in-state education with visible positions of responsibility in their home states. These positions built their brand and reinforced their credentials as public leaders. They served as strategic stepping-stones to a governorship, demonstrating what a unique asset an in-state education can provide to a young politician. Consider just a few more examples.

After earning his undergraduate degree in agricultural economics at Kansas State University and his law degree at the University of Kansas, Sam Brownback became Kansas Secretary of Agriculture. Following her graduation from Oklahoma State University, Governor Mary Fallin was elected—to three consecutive terms as lieutenant governor of Oklahoma. Phil Bryant, governor of Mississippi, went to community college, undergraduate school, and graduate school in Mississippi before being elected a state representative, state auditor and lieutenant governor. In between terms as governor of Iowa, Terry Branstad—who earned both his undergraduate and law degrees from Iowa universities—served as the president of Des Moines University.

What They Studied

Moving from the question of where they attended college to what they studied in college, governors show another pattern that, as we will see later, is shared with big-city mayors. Governors' selection of college majors was dominated by the social sciences, with more than 40 percent opting for a course of study such as political science, economics, or psychology. This was followed by the humanities (history, English, classics), which were tied with business, and accounting at 17 percent as a distant second for most popular choice. Only four governors majored in a STEM curriculum as undergraduates.

Postgraduate Study

Thirty-six of the governors (72 percent) earned a graduate or professional degree. Three of them—Raimondo (Rhode Island), Wolf (Pennsylvania), and Snyder (Michigan)—each earned two advanced degrees.

Far and away, the most popular terminal was the JD, earned by twenty-five (69 percent) of the governors with a postgraduate degree. Next in popularity was the MBA (seven), followed by a master's (two), PhD or DPhil (two), and MD (one). Other than John Hickenlooper's MS in geology, no governor obtained a graduate degree in a STEM field, and none of them earned a terminal degree in the humanities.

Private institutions awarded twenty-two (59 percent) of the governors' postgraduate degrees, a 7 percent larger share than with their undergraduate degrees. Similar to their undergraduate education, almost half of the governors (seventeen of thirty-six) earned their advanced degree at an in-state institution. Thirteen of the governors' terminal degrees were awarded by top-ranked universities.

The fact that the majority of all degrees earned by governors were awarded by private institutions might be a little surprising given that overall, many more people enroll in public as opposed to private institutions. According to the most recent figures, about 80 percent of the students entering college in the fall semester enroll in a public institution. But this pattern does not hold for elected CEOs.

As it turns out, the tendency to attend private more often than public institutions for graduate studies is one of the more consistent preferences found among leading American executives, regardless of whether they are in the public or private sector. In fact, as we will see, this pattern is found in all but one of our executive groupings, that exception being the military leaders.

What other conclusions can we draw about the education of governors? Do they walk a typical educational pathway? Is there a preferred pedigree? Here are three takeaways that stand out.

First, combining undergraduate and graduate institutions, thirty-one (62 percent) of the governors attended at least one of their in-state universities or colleges. As we shall see later, governors share this educational characteristic with our sample of mayors: they tend, more than any of the other executive types, to have earned their degrees from institutions from within their home states. Other than mayors and governors, we do not see anywhere near this degree of state centricity in the other executive groups.

This concentration of in-state alma maters may simply reflect the state loyalty that one finds among many students, or even more practically, the economic advantage associated with paying the lower tuition charged to in-state students. More likely, as already discussed, studying at in-state institutions conveys several strategic benefits to budding politicians.

Whatever the reason, claiming an in-state alma mater is not likely to be harmful to candidates aspiring to statewide elected office. Perhaps the nascent notion of eventually pursuing a political career is tied to the idea that listing a state institution on one's resume will be an electoral bonus.

Second, the predominance of lawyers reflects a common career trajectory in the histories of governors. Many had previously served in the office of the state attorney general, for which a law degree is a requirement. Steve Bullock from Nevada; Jerry Brown in California; New York's Andrew Cuomo; and Brian Sandoval, governor of Nevada, all served a term as their state's attorney general before becoming governor. Gregg Abbott served on the Texas Supreme Court and was elected Texas attorney general before becoming the governor of Texas. And as we have already seen, Missouri's Jay Nixon was

elected attorney general four times in his state before going on to become one
of only four governors to be elected to successive terms in Missouri.

Several other governors parlayed their JDs into highly visible legal positions prior to becoming their state's elected CEO. After graduating from
Seton Hall University School of Law, Chris Christie was appointed US
attorney for New Jersey by George W. Bush in 2002. Bush also appointed
Matt Mead to a US attorney position in Wyoming after Mead had earned his
JD from the University of Wyoming. Although she earned her law degree at
the University of Oklahoma, Susana Martinez served three terms as a district
attorney in Dona Ana County, New Mexico, before being elected that state's
governor. And of course, several lawyers-cum-governors had been earlier
elected to their state legislatures (Brown in Oregon and Daugaard in South
Dakota) or the US Congress (Deal in Georgia and Pence in Indiana), public
offices for which a career as a lawyer is helpful as well as common.

Finally, the largest percentage of governors graduated with an undergraduate degree in the social sciences. Only four governors earned degrees in the
fields of math, engineering, or the sciences, and a mere eight majored in the
humanities. By far, the single most common major was political science or
some variant of it such as government or American studies. The sciences and
humanities were also almost completely absent in governors' postgraduate
education, which was dominated by legal training.

To the extent that there is a core knowledge and basic way of thinking
about the process of governing a state that would be useful for a governor, a
major like political science or economics would be an obvious preparation.
They are logical choices that are grounded in practical relevance. But they
also are limiting ones that may impose narrow and predictable perspectives.

This is not the place to argue the relative merits of studying one kind of
academic discipline versus another. But it is worth asking about the implications of what turns out to be a fairly one-sided educational history among
current governors.

The social science lens is not the only way to look at the world, even for
those who are leading state government. It tends to possess less of the empirical rigor, precise measurements, and technical demands of the physical or
biological sciences. These are methods that are keys to discovery and innovation, to new products and advanced technologies.

The humanities are less empirical in methodology than the social sciences,
relying instead on intense speculation and criticism along with a deep understanding of history as their habits of scholarship. The result should be, and
often is, a richer understanding of one's own interior as well as a well-tuned
empathy for the triumphs and tragedies of others.

These are generalizations to be sure, but the fact that our elected CEOs
are, by their educational histories, not highly conversant in the subject matter

and epistemology of either the humanities or the sciences must be of some consequence.

In the words of a former governor, Edwin Edwards: "Without the humanities to teach us how history has succeeded or failed in directing the fruits of technology and science to the betterment of *homo sapiens*, without the humanities to teach us how to frame the discussion and properly debate the uses—and the costs—of technology, without the humanities to teach us how to safely debate how to create a more just society with our fellow man and woman, technology and science would eventually default to the ownership of—and misuse by—the most influential, the most powerful, the most feared among us."[5]

Whatever advantages or disadvantages accompany the primacy of social science and legal education among the governors—and the mayors to whom we turn next—it is a distinguishing feature. For every other CEO group, the humanities and/or the sciences figure more prominently in their educational histories.

MAYORS

Among the mayors of America's fifty largest cities in 2016, forty-seven completed a college degree. Only the mayors of El Paso, Wichita, and Miami were not college graduates.

The fifty mayors earned a total of eighty-five baccalaureate, graduate, and professional degrees. Table 2.2 lists all the mayors and their earned degrees.

Undergraduate Study

The mayors tended to earn their undergraduate degrees more often from private institutions (60 percent). This figure is a bit higher than for our governors, 52 percent of whom attended private undergraduate institutions. Only three institutions graduated more than one mayor—Boston College, Bryn Mawr, and Virginia Commonwealth University, each claiming two.

As with the governors, the range of undergraduate institutions from which big-city mayors graduated is substantial. Included are major research universities (Indiana University, University of Oklahoma, Texas Tech University), highly selective national liberal arts colleges (Kenyon, Sarah Lawrence, and Oberlin), small liberal arts schools (Hastings College and Earlham College), regional and urban campuses (Cleveland State University and California State University campuses at both Fresno and Long Beach), and a historically black institution (Howard University).

Table 2.2   Mayors' Education

City	Mayor	Undergraduate Degree	Graduate Degree
New York City	Bill de Blasio	BA Metropolitan Studies New York U.	Master of International Affairs Columbia
Los Angles	Eric M. Garcetti	BA Political Science/Urban Planning Columbia	Master of International Affairs Columbia
Chicago	Rahm I. Emanuel	BA Liberal Arts Sarah Lawrence College	MA Speech & Communications Northwestern
Houston	Sylvester Turner	BA Political Science U. Houston	JD Harvard
Philadelphia	James F. Kenney	BA Political Science La Salle U.	
San Antonio	Ivy R. Taylor	BA American Studies Yale	
San Diego	Kevin L. Faulconer	BA Political Science San Diego State U.	MA City Planning U. North Carolina
Dallas	Mike S. Rawlings	BA Communications & Philosophy Boston College	
San Jose	Samuel T. Liccardo	BA Government & Economics Georgetown U.	MA Public Policy & JD Harvard
Austin	Steven I. Adler	BA Public and International Affairs Princeton	JD U. Texas
Indianapolis	Joseph H. Hogsett	BA History & Political Science Indiana U.	MA Theological Studies Christian Theological Seminary MA English Butler U. MA History & JD Indiana U.
Jacksonville	Leonard B. Curry	BS Accounting U. Florida	
San Francisco	Edwin M. Lee	BA Government & Legal Studies Bowdoin College	JD U. California (Berkeley)
Columbus	Andrew J. Ginther	BA Political Science Earlham College	
Charlotte	Jennifer W. Roberts	BA English Lit & Math U. North Carolina	MA European History U. Toronto MAIA European Studies Johns Hopkins
Fort Worth	Betsy Price	BS Biology U. Texas (Arlington)	
Detroit	Michael E. Duggan	BA Political Science U. Michigan	JD U. Michigan
El Paso	Oscar Lesser		
Memphis	Jim Strickland	BBA Finance U. Memphis	JD U. Memphis
Seattle	Edward B. Murray	BA Sociology U. Portland	
Denver	Michael B. Hancock	BA Political Science Hastings College	MA Public Admin. & Management U. Colorado (Denver)
Washington, DC	Muriel E. Bowser	BA History Chatham College	MA Public Policy American U.

City	Name		
Boston	Martin J. Walsh	BA Political Science Boston College	MBA Vanderbilt U.
Nashville	Megan C. Barry	BA Elementary Educ. Baker U.	JD U. Michigan
Phoenix	Gregory J. Stanton	BA History & Political Science Marquette U.	JD U. Maryland
Baltimore	Stephanie Rawlings-Blake	BA Political Science Oberlin College	MBA New York U.
Oklahoma City	Mick Cornett	BA Journalism U. Oklahoma	
Louisville	Greg E. Fischer	BA Economics Vanderbilt U.	
Portland	Charles A. Hales	BA Political Theory U. Virginia	
Las Vegas	Carolyn G. Goodman	BA Anthropology Bryn Mawr College	MA Counseling U. Nevada (Law Vegas)
Milwaukee	Thomas M. Barrett	BA Economics U. Wisconsin	JD U. Wisconsin
Albuquerque	Richard J. Berry	BA Finance & Administration U. New Mexico	
Tucson	Jonathan Rothschild	BS Kenyon College	JD U. New Mexico
Fresno	Ashley E. Swearengin	BS Marketing California State U. (Fresno)	MBA California State U. (Fresno)
Sacramento	Kevin M. Johnson	BA Political Science U. California (Berkeley)	
Long Beach	Robert Garcia	BA Communication Studies California State U. (Long Beach)	MA Communication Management U. Southern California EdD Education Policy California State U. (Long Beach)
Kansas City	Sylvester "Sly" James	BA English Rockhurst U.	JD U. Minnesota
Mesa	John Giles	BA Political Sciences Brigham Young U.	JD Arizona State U.
Virginia Beach	William D. Sessoms Jr.	BA Business Admin. Virginia Commonwealth U.	
Atlanta	Mohammed Kassin Reed	BA Political Science Howard U.	JD Howard U.
Colorado Springs	John W. Suthers	BA Government U. Notre Dame	JD U. Colorado
Omaha	Jean Stothert	BS Nursing Seattle Pacific U.	
Raleigh	Nancy McFarlane	BS Pharmacy Virginia Commonwealth U.	
Miami	Tomas P. Regalado	Attended U. Miami	
Oakland	Elizabeth B. Schaaf	BA Political Science Rollins College	JD Loyola U (Los Angeles)
Minneapolis	Elizabeth A. Hodges	BA Psychology & Sociology Bryn Mawr College	MA Sociology U. Wisconsin
Tulsa	Dewey F. Bartlett Jr.	BS Accounting Regis U.	MBA Southern Methodist U.
Cleveland	Frank G. Jackson	BA Urban Studies & History Cleveland State U.	MA Urban Affairs & JD Cleveland State U.
Wichita	Jeff Longwell	Attended Wichita State U.	
Arlington	Jeff Williams	BS Civil Engineering Texas Tech U.	

Thirteen of the mayors were awarded their undergraduate degrees from one of the institutions designated as top-ranked (i.e., a *U.S. News* top twenty national or public university or a top ten national liberal arts college). Only three mayors received their undergraduate degrees from an Ivy League school. Recall that eight governors had done so. Of the forty-seven mayors with an undergraduate degree, almost three-quarters of them earned it from a college that did not occupy a lofty position in the *U.S. News* rankings.

Mayors and governors were similar in two notable respects: they shared the tendency to graduate from an institution located in the state in which they were later elected, and mayors' selection of undergraduate majors was also highly concentrated in the social sciences.

Twenty-one (45 percent) of the college graduate mayors earned their degrees from an in-state institution. Even more remarkable is the number of mayors who attended college in the very city they would later lead.

Most of America's major cities are home to one or more fine higher education institutions, and more than one-quarter of our mayors stayed close to home and attended one of their own city's institutions for their undergraduate studies. The histories of Memphis mayor Jim Strickland and Frank G. Jackson, mayor of Cleveland, illustrate this pattern well.

After moving to Memphis with his family when he was twelve, Jim Strickland attended famed Christian Brothers High School. While there, he edited the high school yearbook and attended a lot of sporting events at the nearby University of Memphis, then known as Memphis State University. After graduation, he enrolled at the University of Memphis and immediately became involved in student government, first as a senator and by his senior year, as student class president. He also interned for two local representatives who were serving in the Tennessee state legislature.

A finance major at the University of Memphis, Strickland enrolled in the university's law school immediately after graduation. By the time he graduated from law school, he had worked on dozens of political campaigns at both the state and municipal levels and had become a well-known figure in Memphis politics. Just five years out of law school and practicing law in Memphis, he became the Shelby County Democratic Party chairman. He lost his first bid to be elected to the Memphis City Council but won a seat two years later and continued on the city council for seven consecutive years, until his election to mayor in 2015.

Strickland's attendance at the University of Memphis allowed him to become an established political leader in the city at an early age. Could he have done so if he had gone away to school and then returned to Memphis to practice law and pursue elected office? Perhaps, but it is doubtful that he would have made anywhere near the party connections or earned the local loyalties that are both so crucial to being elected a big-city mayor.

The same is true of Frank Jackson, now in his third term as mayor of Cleveland. Jackson grew up in one of Cleveland's poorest neighborhoods and attended the city's public schools. He struggled early in school and was held back in both the third and sixth grades. But education ultimately proved to be Jackson's road to success. After graduating from Max S. Hayes High School and serving in the army in Vietnam, he returned to his Cleveland neighborhood and went on to earn four degrees—an associate's degree at Cuyahoga Community College and a BA, MA, and JD, all from Cleveland State University.

Jackson's first job after law school was as an assistant city prosecutor in Cleveland, and in 1989 he was elected to his first term on the Cleveland City Council. He served on the council for sixteen years, representing Cleveland's Fifth Ward. In 2002, he was elected council president, and in 2005 he won his first campaign to be the mayor of Cleveland. Still a resident of his old childhood neighborhood, Mayor Jackson is the prototype of the homegrown, locally educated mayor.

What They Studied

Almost two-thirds of big-city mayors majored in political science, sociology, economics, government, metropolitan studies, or a dual major in which one of the disciplines was a social science. In fact, social science majors were twice as numerous as all the other majors combined. A total of three mayors graduated with a degree in the humanities, and five earned a STEM degree, defined in their cases to include biology, civil engineering, nursing, pharmacy, and a dual concentration in English literature and mathematics.

This concentration on the social sciences is accompanied by another aspect of mayors' backgrounds that may be even more important to their careers than the major they selected. In many cases, majoring in political science or government meant that those students had a practicum or internship where they worked in the office of a public official. They got the chance to serve as an apprentice to someone who showed them how a campaign is organized, how an ordinance gets passed, and how a public policy is shaped. They learned the nuts and bolts of a city's executive departments, the ins and outs of the personnel system, the give and take of labor negotiations. Often, the internship led to a first job in the office of a local official.

James Kenney, mayor of Philadelphia, is a great example of this trajectory. While still a junior at LaSalle University, he interned for State Senator Vince Fumo, whose district office was in South Philly. Immediately after Kenney's graduation, Fumo hired him onto his staff. Kenney's political career was off and running.

Although he went away to Hastings College in Nebraska for his undergraduate studies, Denver native Michael Hancock returned home every summer to work as an intern in the office of Mayor Frederico Pena. After graduating from Hastings, Hancock returned to Denver for good. He attended the University of Colorado at Denver, working at two jobs—at the Denver Housing Authority and the National Civic League—while earning his master's in public administration. In 2003 he was elected to the Denver City Council, and in 2011, following in his mentor's footsteps, Hancock became the forty-fifth mayor of Denver.

Born in New Jersey, but raised in Fulton County, Georgia, Kasim Reed attended Howard University, a private, historically black university in Washington, DC. While majoring in political science at Howard, he interned for Joseph P. Kennedy II, who represented the Eighth Congressional District in Massachusetts, a seat previously held by "Tip" O'Neill and before him, Joe's uncle, former President John F. Kennedy.

While interning for Kennedy, Kasim learned how federal matching programs operated, and he decided to see if he could get one implemented at Howard. He proposed a $15 per-semester student-fee increase that would be matched by federal contributions on a dollar-for-dollar basis. The resulting fund would then be used to boost the university's endowment.

Reed was in a good position to push his idea because he was the student representative to Howard's Board of Trustees. It was on Howard's board where he met former Atlanta mayor Andrew Young, who was a Howard trustee at the time. Reed gave a sales pitch for the matching fund idea to Young, who was skeptical that it could work. But several million dollars later, a now-grateful Andrew Young is reported to have told Reed to come back to Atlanta and "run for something."[6] Reed did. At the age of twenty-nine, he was elected to the Georgian general assembly. Four years later, in 2002, he won his race for the Georgia senate. And in 2013, he was reelected to a second term as mayor of Atlanta, winning more than 90 percent of the vote.

Kenney, Hancock, and Reed were all able to craft highly personal, professionally relevant college experiences that propelled them toward their political successes. As important as their formal classroom studies might have been, as inspiring as the many outstanding lecturers they probably heard, their most formative lessons occurred outside a classroom, where they found, or were discovered by, a trusted mentor. They encountered an experienced professional with whom they developed an intensive, deep relationship, someone who served as their secure anchor. And with the guidance and encouragement of this steadfast advisor, they started taking steps toward the life they had imagined.

These mentorships were cited in chapter 1 as the kind of campus experiences that graduates looked back on years later as the most important dimension of their college education. Relationships that challenged them, that pushed or pulled them to set their sights just a little bit higher.

It should come as no surprise that these same personal relationships loom large in the preparation of many of our elected CEOs. Think of them as "but for" experiences: "but for" meeting this person, I would never have had the confidence to start out in politics; "but for" this faculty's encouragement, I would have dropped out of school.

Postgraduate Study

Thirty-one mayors (62 percent) earned a graduate degree of some kind, and five of them earned more than one. Jospeh Hogsett, the mayor of Indianapolis has four advanced degrees to his credit, including a JD and separate master's degrees in history, English, and theological studies. Jennifer Roberts, the mayor of Charlotte; Sam Liccardo of San Jose; Frank Jackson in Cleveland; and Long Beach's Robert Garcia each earned two graduate degrees.

As with the governors, the most popular degree was the JD, which was earned by seventeen (55 percent) of the mayors with an advanced degree. Next most popular was a master's degree usually in a policy field such as international affairs, city planning, or public administration, earned by nine (29 percent) of the mayors. Four mayors received an MBA, and one—Robert Garcia of Long Beach—received an EdD. The only two mayors to earn humanities degrees were Jennifer Roberts with an MA in European history from the University of Toronto and an MAIA in European studies from Johns Hopkins, and Joseph Hogsett with an MA in English from Butler University and an MA in history from Indiana University. Not a single mayor earned a graduate STEM degree.

Public institutions granted twenty-one (57 percent) of the total thirty-seven graduate degrees earned by mayors, an almost mirror reversal of the larger share of mayors' undergraduate degrees having been earned from private institutions. Of the mayors holding a graduate or professional degree, nineteen earned it from an institution in the state where they were elected mayor, and fifteen earned it from one of the fifty-three top-ranked institutions.

To sum up, the average big-city mayor was educated close to home with an undergraduate major in a social science, followed by an advanced degree in legal or policy studies.

- Combining undergraduate with graduate degrees, thirty-two of the mayors graduated from at least one of their home-state institutions.
- Two-thirds majored in one of the disciplines traditionally defined as a social science.
- Of the thirty-one mayors with an advanced degree, twenty-three, or 74 percent, received either a JD or a master's in a field such as urban planning, sociology, or public administration.

Being the elected CEO of a local or state government is basically an exercise in how to organize and direct cooperation so that public business can be accomplished. The individuals considered in this chapter, selected by the public to lead a government, tended to prepare themselves in a very pragmatic fashion for the political careers they sought.

Our elected CEOs—governors and mayors—were not, for the most part, educated at America's top-ranked colleges. Fewer than 15 percent earned an MBA. Neither the humanities nor the sciences were prominent in their backgrounds. Instead, they obtained an education that was eminently practical for their political careers. It maximized their exposure to their eventual constituents. It enabled them to learn and strengthen political skills, often at the side of a seasoned mentor. It equipped them with the basic knowledge for the job of governance.

NOTES

1. http://www.daytondailynews.com/news/state--regional-govt--politics/kasich-letter-nixon-released-for-first-time/law9aI9wFoqqCxMTCIAufK/

2. Ibid.

3. Ibid.

4. http://daily.kellogg.edu/2014/09/22/kcc-awards-degree-to-governor-rick-snyder/

5. http://www.academia.edu/8919778/Introductory_remarks_by_former_four-term_Louisiana_Governor_Edwin_W._Edwards_Honorary_Chair_Montreal_Enlightenment_Conference_October_18_2014

6. http://www.ajc.com/news/things-you-need-know-about-atlanta-mayor-kasim-reed/ZndRBcIWb1imDBcA5BvPHP/

Chapter 3

Dow 30 and Fortune 500 CEOs

Born in Pineville, Kentucky, Rodney McMullen moved to southwest Ohio with his parents, William and Henrietta. Rodney was still a young boy, but his folks worked in factories, and they had to move to wherever they could find the best jobs. By the time Rodney was in high school, the family returned to Kentucky, taking up residence in Williamstown, a town of about 4,000 people, due south of Cincinnati by about forty miles. They lived a frugal life, according to McMullen. "My parents had the kind of jobs where if the economy went soft, you got laid off. You don't want anyone to have the fear I had growing up."[1]

Rodney graduated from Williamstown High School and, with the encouragement of his parents, decided he needed to go to college so he could have a chance at a more prosperous and stable future. The only school he gave much thought to was the University of Kentucky, in Lexington, right down I-75. Rodney was like a lot of kids from rural Kentucky who dreamed of going to UK largely because of the success of the Wildcats, the winningest college basketball program in history. Parked in a car on a hillside in eastern Kentucky or hunched over the radio in the family kitchen, kids from that era tuned in to hear the unmistakable voice of Caywood Ledford call every UK Wildcats game. Caywood was one of the best student recruiters the University of Kentucky ever had.

In 1978, at the age of seventeen, Rodney enrolled at UK. To make ends meet and pay for his tuition he took a part-time job at the Kroger grocery store in the Eastland Shopping Center. He did whatever jobs the store needed to be done—running the cash register, bagging groceries, and stocking the shelves. Years later he told a reporter, "I worked every job in that store, from the dairy to the deli."[2]

One of Lexington's first shopping centers, Eastland is just a couple of miles from the UK campus. Rodney knew the route well, working all the different shifts at Kroger's to pay his way through school. That Kroger store is no longer there. It was replaced by a Save-A-Lot, but the neighborhood remains much the same—a hodgepodge of laundromats, auto supply stores, and discount shops.

It took Rodney only four years to earn both his bachelor's and master's degrees in accounting from UK. And he continued to discover more about Kroger. "I learned a lot," he says. "Of course, I learned a little of everything about our business, which was invaluable. But more importantly, I learned about hard work. . . . It was an experience I wouldn't give up."[3]

After graduation, McMullen stayed on with Kroger's, working first in a division office in Charlotte for four years before moving to company headquarters in Cincinnati, to be a financial analyst. In 1995 Rodney was named Kroger's chief financial officer, and he became the company's chief operating officer in 2009.

In 2014, thirty-six years after starting as a stock boy, Rodney McMullen was named the CEO of the Kroger Company, a $100 billion corporation and the largest traditional supermarket chain in the nation. Kroger gave him the key to the store he started at in Lexington. He still keeps it in his corporate office.

This chapter surveys the education of forty-nine other individuals, who, like Rodney McMullen, have climbed to the highest rung on America's corporate ladder. All of them lead a Fortune 500 company. This sample includes the CEOs of the thirty companies listed on the Dow Jones Industrial Average plus the leaders of the next twenty largest corporations not listed on the Dow.

These are men and women of extraordinary power and influence. They are the leaders of the nation's largest and most profitable enterprises across a broad range of industries—technology, retail, health care, media, and large manufacturers. They are the first group of CEOs in the private sector to be reviewed, giving us an opportunity to see if the educational patterns found with our public sector CEOs generalize to a different group of leaders.

EDUCATIONAL HISTORY

All of the sample of Fortune 500 CEOs earned a college degree. Twenty-six of them earned a postgraduate degree. Table 3.1 presents the CEOs and their degrees.

Let's consider this one basic fact just a bit more: all of these fifty CEOs graduated from college. Every one of them. Skeptics about the value of college love to hold up individuals like Bill Gates or Steve Jobs and use them as examples for the claim that a college degree is not necessary for success in business.

Gates, the richest man in the world, quit Harvard after two years and founded Microsoft. Jobs attended Reed College for about six months, dropped out, and then unofficially sat in on whatever classes he fancied for about eighteen months. Just a few years later, in 1976, he founded Apple along with his friend Steve Wozniak.

Gates and Jobs are not typical people. They both had exceptional talents. Gates scored 1,590 out of a possible 1,600 on the SAT. While at Harvard, he devised a solution to previously unsolved math problems and collaborated with a Harvard computer science professor to publish the results. Jobs was a genius hippie whose uncanny ability in electronics and creative thinking about technology enabled him to become an extraordinary inventor. They were geeks par excellence. But to suggest that their highly unusual paths to success are a preferred or reasonable career strategy over earning a college degree simply ignores the evidence. It's like pointing (down) to Muggsy Bogues and saying that being tall is not important in the NBA.

Gates, himself, recognized the value of a college education. In a 2015 blog-post, he wrote, "Although I dropped out of college and got lucky pursuing a career in software, getting a degree is a much surer path to success. College graduates are more likely to find a rewarding job, earn higher income, and even, evidence shows, live healthier lives than if they didn't have degrees. It's just too bad that we're not producing more of them. As the class of 2015 prepares to join the workforce, what many people may not realize is that America is facing a shortage of college graduates."[4]

Even though he dropped out of college, Jobs still credited Reed with having an invaluable influence on him. Speaking at the 2005 Stanford commencement, Jobs reminisced about a class he audited after officially withdrawing:

> Much of what I stumbled into by following my curiosity and intuition turned out to be priceless later on . . . Reed College at that time offered perhaps the best calligraphy instruction in the country. Throughout the campus every poster, every label on every drawer, was beautifully hand calligraphed. Because I had dropped out and didn't have to take the normal classes, I decided to take a cal-ligraphy class to learn how to do this. I learned about serif and sans serif type-faces, about varying the amount of space between different letter combinations, about what makes great calligraphy great. It was beautiful, historical, artistically subtle in a ways that science can't capture, and I found it fascinating.
>
> None of this had even a hope of any practical application in my life. But 10 years later, when we were designing the first Macintosh computer, it all came back to me. And we designed it all into the Mac. It was the first computer with beautiful typography. If I had never dropped in on that single course in college, the Mac would have never had multiple typefaces or proportionally spaced

Table 3.1　DOW 30/Fortune 500 CEOs' Education

CEO	Company	Undergraduate Degree	Graduate Degree
Inge G. Thulin	3M Company	BA Economics & Marketing U. Gothenburg	
Kenneth I. Chenault	American Express	BA History Bowdoin College	JD Harvard
Timothy D. Cook	Apple	BS Industrial Eng. Auburn U.	MBA Duke
Dennis A. Muilenburg	Boeing	BS Aerospace Engineering Iowa State U.	MS Aeronautics & Astronautics U. Washington
Douglas R. Oberhelman	Caterpillar	BA Finance Milliken College	
John S. Watson	Chevron	BA Ag. Economics U. California (Davis)	MBA U. Chicago
Charles H. Robbins	Cisco	BS Mathematical Sciences U. North Carolina	
Ahmet Muhtar Kent	Coca-Cola	BS Economics U. Hull	
Robert A. Iger	Disney	BS Television and Radio Ithaca College	
Edward D. Breen	DuPont	BS Business Admin. Grove City College	
Rex W. Tillerson	Exxon Mobil	BS Civil Engineering U. Texas	
Jeffrey R. Immelt	General Electric	BA Applied Mathematics & Economics Dartmouth	MBA Harvard
Lloyd C. Blankfein	Goldman Sachs	BA History Harvard	JD Harvard
Craig A. Menear	Home Depot	BA Personnel Admin. Michigan State U.	
Virginia M. "Ginni" Rometty	IBM	BS Computer Science & Electrical Engineering Northwestern	
Alex Gorsky	Johnson & Johnson	BS Engineering & Political Science US Military Academy	MBA U. Pennsylvania
James Dimon	JPMorgan Chase	BA Psychology & Economics Tufts U.	MBA Harvard
Stephen J. Easterbrook	McDonald's	BS Natural Sciences Durham U.	
Kenneth Frazier	Merck	BA Political Science Pennsylvania State U.	JD Harvard
Mark Parker	Nike	BA Political Science Pennsylvania State U.	
Ian C. Read	Pfizer	BS Chemical Engineering Imperial College London	
David S. Taylor	Proctor & Gamble	BS Electrical Engineering Duke	
Alan D. Schnitzer	Travelers	BS Accounting & Finance U. Pennsylvania	JD Columbia

Name	Company	Bachelor's Degree	Advanced Degree(s)
Satya Nadella	Microsoft	BS Electrical Engineering Manipal Institute of Technology	MS Computer Science U. Wisconsin (Milwaukee) MBA U. Chicago
Gregory J. Hayes	United Technologies	BS Economics Purdue U.	
Stephen J. Hemsley	UnitedHealth Group	BA Accounting Fordham U.	
Lowell C. McAdam	Verizon	BS Engineering Cornell	MBA U. San Diego
Charles W. Scharf	VISA	BA Johns Hopkins U.	MBA New York U.
Carl D. "Doug" McMillon	Walmart	BS Business Admin. U. Arkansas	MBA U. Tulsa
Warren E. Buffett	Berkshire Hathaway	BS Business Admin. U. Nebraska	MS Economics Columbia
John H. Hammergren	McKesson	BA Business Admin. U. Minnesota	MBA Xavier U. (Cincinnati)
Larry J. Merlo	CVS Health	BS Pharmacy U. Pittsburgh	
Mary T. Barra	General Motors	BS Electrical Eng. Kettering U.	MBA Stanford
Mark Fields	Ford	BA Economics Rutgers U.	MBA Harvard
Randall L. Stephenson	AT&T	BS Accounting U. Central Oklahoma	MBA U. Oklahoma
Steven H. Collis	AmerisourceBergen	Bachelors of Commerce U. Witwatersand	
W. Craig Jelinek	Costco	BA Business San Diego State U.	
Timothy J. Mayopoulos	Fannie Mae	BA English Cornell	JD New York U.
William R. McMullen	Kroger	BS Accounting BBA Finance U. Kentucky	MS Accounting U. Kentucky
Jeff Bezos	Amazon	BS Electrical Eng. & Computer Science Princeton U.	
Stephano Pessina	Walgreen Boots Alliance	BS Nuclear Eng. Polytechnic University of Milan	
Dion J. Weisler	Hewlett Packard	BS Computing Monash U. (Australia)	
George S. Barrett	Cardinal Health	BA Music & History Brown	MBA New York U.
Timothy C. Wentworth	Express Scripts	BS Industrial & Labor Relations Cornell	
Brian T. Moynihan	Bank of America	BA History Brown	JD Notre Dame
John G. Stumpf	Wells Fargo	BA Finance St. Cloud State U.	MBA U. Minnesota
Michael L. Corbat	Citigroup	BA Economics Harvard	
Greg C. Garland	Phillips 66	BS Chemical Eng. Texas A&M U.	
Joseph W. Gorder	Valero Energy	BBA Accounting U. Missouri (St. Louis)	MBA Our Lady of the Lake U.
Brian M. Krzanich	Intel	BS Chemistry San Jose State U.	

fonts. And since Windows just copied the Mac, it's likely that no personal computer would have had them. If I had never dropped out, I would have never dropped in on this calligraphy class, and personal computers might not have the wonderful typography they do. Of course, it was impossible to connect the dots looking forward when I was in college. But it was very, very clear looking backward 10 years later.[5]

UNDERGRADUATE STUDIES

A majority (twenty-nine) of the CEOs attended a public college for their undergraduate education. This includes seven public universities located outside of the United States, which is the first characteristic that sets the education of this group apart.

Where They Studied

Our Dow 30/Fortune 500 sample is the only CEO group where a sizable number of individuals were educated in countries other than the United States. All told, eight of the CEOs pursued their undergraduate education overseas. Muhtar Kent (Coca-Cola), Steve Easterbrook (McDonald's), and Ian Read (Pfizer) graduated from colleges in England. The other five international alumni are AmerisourceBergen's Steven Collis (South Africa), 3M's Inge Thulin (Sweden), Walgreen's Stefano Pessina (Italy), Hewlett Packard's Dion Weisler (Australia), and Microsoft's Satya Nadella (India).

For decades, America's higher education system has been envied by almost every other country in the world. The number of international students who come to the United States for their college education continues to grow. In 2016, more than one million international students studied at American colleges and universities, an all-time record. According to data from the Institute of International Education, more than 425,000 international undergraduates attended US four-year colleges in 2016, almost 2.5 times the number who attended in 2005.[6] Contrast this figure with the 314,000 American students who studied abroad during this same period, and you understand that the United States remains a large net importer of college students, many of whom remain in America after graduation and join our labor force.

But this trend is accompanied by other interacting realities: large American companies do a great deal of business outside the United States, and these same companies are very willing to go global in their search for talent and leadership. Foreign sales account for about one-third of the total revenue of the S&P 500 companies, a very healthy figure in light of recent market and geopolitical unrest, particularly in Europe and Asia.

Hiring a CEO who brings a cosmopolitan perspective and multicultural competence to company leadership is a smart strategy for many reasons, not the least of which is realizing a better bottom line. It is also a strategy that has been recognized by authors like Thomas Friedman, who in his highly influential *The World Is Flat*[7] and *Thank You for Being Late*,[8] pointed to outsourcing, offshoring, and open-source information sharing as forces that are requiring most businesses to become more global in their outlook and search for leadership.

A 2014 study of all the Fortune 500 companies in the United States revealed that 14 percent were headed by CEOs who were not native born in the United States.[9] This figure is very close to the 16 percent of our Dow 30/Fortune 500 sample who received their undergraduate education outside of the United States.

Twenty (40 percent) of these CEOs completed their undergraduate studies at one of the institutions on the top-ranked list. The fact that the majority of the CEOs in this very exclusive group were not educated at one of America's elite colleges is interesting in itself and is consistent with the overall findings of the book.

Perhaps more remarkable is that a number of these companies have a history of being led by executives who were educated at local or regional colleges that have never been regarded as highly selective, elite, or particularly prestigious. This current sample of executives is not an aberration. Several Dow 30 businesses have made a habit of appointing CEOs who were educated at state and regional universities or small colleges, whose main appeal appears largely to have been that they were located close to where the person grew up.

Let's start with the largest company in the world, Walmart. With annual sales topping $480 billion, if Walmart were a country, it would rank in the top thirty in the world for GDP. It employs more than 2.2 million "associates" and operates more than 11,500 stores in over thirty-five countries. Its succession of CEOs illustrates the general principle that the proximity of a college is often much more important than its prestige, at least in the case of the people who have headed up the world's largest company.

Walmart has had only five CEOs, including its founder, Sam Walton, who opened the first official store in Rogers, Arkansas, in 1962. Walton, who served as the company's CEO from its founding until 1988, attended David H. Hickman High School in Columbia, Missouri. After graduation, he stayed right in Columbia and entered the University of Missouri, majoring in economics. He worked his way through school by waiting tables in the student union, working as a lifeguard, and delivering newspapers. His first job after the University of Missouri was with JCPenney, where he earned $75 a month as a management trainee.

Walton was succeeded by David D. Glass, who served as CEO of Walmart from 1988 to 2000. Glass was born in a farmhouse in Oregon County, but grew up in Mountain View, Missouri, a town of fewer than 1,000 people. After Glass finished a tour in the army, he enrolled at what was then called Southwest Missouri State University in Springfield, Missouri, about ninety miles to the northwest (the institution was renamed Missouri State University in 2005).

Working his way through school as an evening dispatcher for a local trucking company, Glass graduated from Missouri State with a degree in accounting in 1960 and took his first job as an accountant for J. W. Crank, a small drugstore chain in Springfield. He moved to Austin, Texas, to build a Howard Johnson's motel and then returned to Missouri to work for the grocery company, Consumers Markets, which is where he first met Sam Walton.

Walton eventually succeeded in recruiting Glass to join Walmart in 1976 as its vice president of finance. Over a decade later, Walton tapped Glass to be his permanent successor and, with that promotion, put in place the individual, who more than anyone else, is credited with developing Walmart's famously successful supply chain model of business.

H. Lee Scott was Walmart's next CEO, taking over for Glass in 2000. Born in Joplin, Missouri, Scott moved with his parents to the small town of Baxter Springs, Kansas. Scott spent much of his youth working at his father's service station. After graduating from high school, Scott attended Pittsburg State University, which was only twenty-five miles north of Baxter Springs. He worked his way through college, making tire molds and earning $1.95 an hour. As a student, he lived with his wife and son in a small trailer. Scott graduated from Pittsburg State in 1971, with a degree in business administration.

His first job out of college was as a trainee with the Yellow Freight System—a Kansas trucking company. In 1997, Yellow Freight transferred Scott to Springdale, Arkansas, where he met David Glass, with whom he had a dispute over a $7,000 bill to Walmart that Glass refused to pay. Despite this argument, Glass liked Scott and offered him a job at a Walmart distribution center. Scott turned him down, but a few years later he was hired to head up Walmart's transportation department. As CEO he is credited with leading Walmart's successful global expansion.

The fourth CEO, Mike Duke, is a bit of an exception to the Walmart CEO mold, but only a little bit. Like Walton, Glass, and Scott before him, Duke stayed close to home to go to college. Unlike his predecessors, however, he went to a very highly ranked college, particularly in the field in which Duke elected to major.

Duke grew up on a farm in Fayette County, Georgia, southwest of Atlanta. His father was a truck driver in Atlanta, and his mother was a stay-at-home mom. Duke was a fiercely competitive athlete in school and also excelled at math and science. In high school, he was elected president of his senior class. His high school physics teacher, Mr. McDaniel, advised him to go to Georgia Tech University and study industrial engineering, which is exactly what Duke did, graduating in 1971. He worked for a few department store chains after graduation, before being recruited to Walmart in 1995 by Scott to be his deputy in charge of logistics. Duke became CEO of Walmart in 2009, a position he held for five years before turning the post over to Douglas McMillon.

McMillon was born in Memphis, spent his early youth in Jonesboro, Arkansas, and then moved to Bentonville at age sixteen so his father could open up his dental practice there. He played point guard for Bentonville High School, and during the summer he unloaded trucks at a local Walmart warehouse. McMillon attended the University of Arkansas in nearby Fayetteville. In the summers, he would return home to work at the Bank of Bentonville.

Soon after graduating from Arkansas with his business administration degree, McMillon enrolled in the University of Tulsa's MBA program. Even before completing his MBA, McMillon started working in Tulsa's Walmart Store #894 as a buyer trainee. He moved to company headquarters in Bentonville a year later, and his big break came in 2005 when he assumed the position of CEO for Sam's Club. After taking over the international division in 2009, McMillon moved up to CEO in 2014.

Born into working or middle class families, humble and down to earth in their demeanors, the Walmart leaders worked their way through school while attending colleges that were all within 100 miles of their homes. None of their alma maters (with the exception of Duke at Georgia Tech) enjoyed any name prestige. In fact, in each case, these five men enrolled in the four-year institution that was the closest geographically to them.

The education of the Walmart CEOs would qualify as an interesting and inspiring story, even if they were the only exceptions to the otherwise robust rule that our major private businesses preferred CEOs who were educated at America's most highly esteemed colleges. But they are far from the sole exception. A very similar pattern can be found at other powerhouse corporations.

Take the case of Valero Energy Corporation, an international manufacturer and distributer of transportation and power. Headquartered in San Antonio, Texas, Valero owns and operates oil refineries across North America, the Caribbean, and the United Kingdom. Valero is the world's largest independent refiner of petroleum, and in 2016 was ranked sixteenth on the Fortune 500 list.

The past three CEOs for Valero have been, in order of earliest to most recent, Bill Greehey, William Klesse, and Joseph Gorder, who began as the current CEO in 2014. Here is where they attended college:

- After a term in the military, during which he was stationed at Lackland Air Force Base in San Antonio, Greehey attended St. Mary's University, where he received his accounting degree in 1960. Greehey was able to afford college through the GI Bill along with the financial aid he received from St. Mary's. If you were to travel to San Antonio and make a visit to the campus of St. Mary's today, you could stop by and tour the Bill Greehey School of Business, established by Mr. Greehey's personal $25 million gift to the school's endowment.
- A native of New Jersey, Klesse attended the University of Dayton, where he was a soccer star and a 1968 graduate in chemical engineering. Klesse then moved to Texas for his job and enrolled in West Texas A&M, located in the small town of Canyon, Texas, fifty miles north of San Antonio. He earned his MBA there in 1973. Klesse, who worked for Valero and related companies for more than forty years, served as CEO from 2005 to 2014.
- Gorder grew up in Maryland Heights, Missouri, a suburb of St. Louis. In 1979, he earned his bachelor's of business administration from the University of Missouri, St. Louis (UMSL), located just minutes from his home. Gorder decided to enroll at UMSL after observing the success his older sister experienced there. "UMSL was the right school for me," he explained in an interview with the school newspaper. "The broad availability of classes made it possible for me to work 30 to 40 hours per week and graduate on time. I could afford it and it was the best value."[10] After moving to San Antonio, Gorder worked as director of information systems for a local oil and gas company. He wanted to earn an MBA so he could advance in his career, but it was difficult for him to do so because he was working more than fifty hours a week and also raising two children. He turned to the nearby Our Lady of the Lake University, which was the first San Antonio area university to offer degree programs on weekends. Attending Our Lady of the Lake's Weekend College allowed Gorder to work during the week and attend classes on the weekend. In 1992, he was awarded his MBA, and more than two decades later he became CEO of Valero.

The list of Dow 30/Fortune 500 CEOs who stayed close to home for their education may not be quite as long as the list for the governors and mayors, but it still is a strong enough finding to be noteworthy.

- At General Motors, Mary Barra earned her undergraduate degree in electrical engineering from Kettering University (formerly the General Motors Institute), located in Flint, Michigan. The daughter of an auto worker and a car buff herself from a very young age, Barra enrolled at the age of eighteen as a co-op student at Kettering before starting her long GM career at the Pontiac, Michigan, plant that built the Fiero.

- Another stay-close-to-home success is Randall Stephenson, the chief executive for AT&T. Stephenson was born in Oklahoma City, graduated from Moore High School, and then earned an accounting degree from the University of Central Oklahoma in Edmond, followed by an MBA from the University of Oklahoma.
- Apple's Tim Cook was born in Robertsdale, Alabama, where he graduated second in his class from the local high school. He stayed in state to attend Auburn University for his industrial engineering degree and remains a die-hard fan of Auburn football.
- Brian Krzanich was born in Santa Clara, California, corporate headquarters for the Intel Corporation. He graduated from nearby San Jose State University in 1982 with a degree in chemistry. Immediately after finishing his degree, he took his first job with Intel as a process engineer at one of the company's chip factories in New Mexico. Several promotions later, he was named CEO of Intel in 2013, continuing the company's forty-year track record of hiring all its CEOs (Krzanich is the sixth) from inside the organization.
- Dennis Muilenburg, chief executive at Boeing, was born on a family farm in the northwest corner of Iowa. He went to Iowa State University, less than 200 miles from home, for his degree in aerospace engineering.
- DuPont CEO Edward Breen was born in Grove City, Pennsylvania, and he stayed in his hometown to attend Grove City College, a small Christian liberal arts school, generally regarded as one of the nation's most politically conservative higher education institutions.
- Warren Buffett, the longtime, iconic CEO of Berkshire Hathaway, was born in Omaha, Nebraska, but moved to Washington, DC, after his father was elected to Congress. At his father's urging, he initially enrolled, while just sixteen years of age, at the highly acclaimed Wharton School of Business at the University of Pennsylvania. But after two years at Penn, Buffett wanted a change and returned to Nebraska, where he earned his economics degree from the University of Nebraska in 1950.

Recalling these experiences years later, Buffett told a group of Nebraska undergrads: "After two years at the Wharton School, I transferred here and I must say that I thought that my year here was considerably superior to either of the years I'd had at Wharton. . . . The teachers turned me on. There wasn't a class that disappointed me."[11]

What They Studied

The Dow 30/Fortune 500 CEOs also stand apart from other groups with respect to their major fields of study. Almost 40 percent (nineteen of the fifty) of the Dow 30/Fortune 500 CEOs earned an undergraduate degree in a STEM field, with engineering being the single most common major. Next most popular was some type of business major, such as business administration, finance, or accounting, with about a third (sixteen) of these CEOs studying those fields. Social sciences were the third most frequent major at 16 percent, and only 10 percent of our Dow 30/Fortune 500 group majored in the humanities.

The prominence of science and engineering degrees reflects the nature of many of the enterprises that dominate the Dow 30. These are America's major manufacturers. They are companies that make things, from cars to computers, aircraft to air conditioners. They generate and distribute power, invent and apply technology, and discover and formulate drugs and medical therapies.

Although having a technical expertise is obviously not a requirement to lead companies such as these, a background in science is certainly an asset for a leader of a company that invents, makes, and applies technologies. Being educated as a scientist or engineer enables a CEO to have a deeper understanding of the core competence of a manufacturing or technology-based company, and it may be an advantage in terms of how the CEO is viewed by others in the organization.

Of the companies in this sample, twenty-six—just over half—focus on a book of business that depends heavily on science or engineering. Included are manufacturers, energy suppliers and distributors, chemical and pharmaceutical companies, and technology developers.

If we confine our attention to just this group of Dow 30/Fortune 500 companies, the importance of a STEM-educated chief executive emerges even more strongly. Sixteen of these science-dependent companies—more than 60 percent—are headed by an individual who earned an undergraduate STEM degree.

GRADUATE STUDIES

Twenty-six of the Dow 30/Fortune 500 CEOs earned an advanced degree of some type. Of this group, twenty-two (85 percent) earned either an MBA (sixteen) or a JD (six). A number of the executives in this group followed up their STEM or social studies degrees as undergraduates with an MBA or a JD at the graduate level. Notable examples include Chevron's John Watson, Jeffrey Immelt at General Electric, Morgan Chase's James Dimon, Satya Nadella with Microsoft, and Ford CEO Mark Fields.

Where They Studied

The list of graduate institutions attended by this group of CEOs is dominated by highly regarded private universities. Twenty of twenty-six earned their highest degree from a private university. More than half of them went to a top-ranked institution, with a third of the group going to one of the Ivy League universities. Harvard led the pack with six graduates, followed by Columbia (two), the University of Chicago (two), and then with one graduate each, Notre Dame, Stanford, Duke, the University of Pennsylvania, and the University of Washington.

This last result is not surprising. The highest-ranked national and public universities earn a significant amount of their prestige because of their large and highly regarded PhD programs and professional schools.

Graduate curricula are generally too expensive or rely too heavily on outside research grants to faculty to be viable at small colleges, regional universities, or metropolitan institutions, so the options for advanced study are narrowed somewhat. Consequently, prestigious universities enroll a larger share of the graduate and professional school populations than they do of undergraduate students.

The tendency for these CEOs to attend top-ranked universities for their graduate education begs another question. Were these executives also more likely to have attended an elite undergraduate school? If so, it would support the belief that graduating from an elite undergraduate institution holds an advantage for being accepted into premier graduate schools. As it turns out, the answer is no. More than half of the CEOs who attended a top-ranked graduate institution did not graduate from an elite undergraduate institution.

The CEOs covered in this chapter are a quintessential group—the leaders of America's largest and most powerful companies. The education of these private sector executives mirrors many of the patterns we found with public sector leaders.

- All of them graduated from college.
- A majority also earned a graduate or professional degree.
- A substantial number attended a college relatively close to home.
- Most of them did not receive their undergraduate degree from one of the country's top-ranked colleges.

There were important differences as well.

- A significant number of our big-business CEOs earned their degrees from foreign universities. It was extremely rare for a public sector CEO to have attended a university outside the United States.
- Nearly 40 percent of these CEOs majored in a STEM field, a much higher percentage than for elected executives who strongly favored the social sciences.

- The majority of Dow 30/Fortune 500 CEOs attended a top-ranked institution for their graduate or professional degree, a substantially higher percentage than with the governors and mayors.
- The MBA was the preferred graduate degree for these CEOs, earned by almost two-thirds of the executives who held an advanced degree. As we shall see, corporate chiefs and media heads are the only executive groups for which the MBA is the dominant graduate degree.

In our next chapter, the education of another group of private sector CEOs, the heads of the country's largest foundations, is considered. This is a group of leaders who are in charge of organizations that make donations rather than profits. They, too, prove to be a well-educated group, but with some surprising differences from other executives.

NOTES

1. http://www.cincinnati.com/story/money/2014/06/25/rodney-mcmullen-took-kroger-top/11387153/
2. Ibid.
3. http://www.ukalumni.net/s/1052/semi-blank-noimg.aspx?sid=1052&gid=1&pgid=4842
4. https://www.gatesnotes.com/Education/11-Million-College-Grads
5. http://singjupost.com/steve-jobs-2005-stanford-commencement-address-full-transcript/2/
6. http://www.iie.org/Research-and-Publications/Open-Doors/Data/International-Students/Academic-Level#.WITLh60zWJA
7. Thomas L. Friedman, *The World Is Flat: A Brief History of the Twenty-First Century* (New York: Farrar, Straus & Giroux, 2005).
8. Thomas L. Friedman, *Thank You for Being Late: An Optimist's Guide to Thriving in the Age of Accelerations* (New York: Farrar, Straus & Giroux, 2016).
9. http://web.boardroominsiders.com/immigrant-ceos-what-global-citizens-bring-to-american-business
10. http://blogs.umsl.edu/news/2014/12/17/gorder/
11. http://www.fool.com/investing/general/2014/11/02/the-surprising-truth-about-warren-buffetts-educati.aspx

Chapter 4

Foundation Executives

The Bill and Melinda Gates Foundation is the largest private foundation in the world, with an endowment of about $40 billion. Launched in 2000 by the richest man in the world, the Gates Foundation has two global priorities: improving health care and reducing poverty and hunger. In the United States, it also focuses on improving K–12 and postsecondary education through technology and other kinds of innovation. The foundation also invests in partnerships with foreign governments, other philanthropists, and policy experts to leverage its reach and success across the globe.

Since its inception, the Gates Foundation has handed out more than $36 billion in grants, and in any given year, it is likely to award $4 billion or more in direct grants to hundreds of recipients. A small sampling of the grants that were awarded in 2016 reveals the breadth of its mission and illustrates the important, in some cases lifesaving, work that a private foundation advances.[1]

- $6 million to promote college completion by low-income, first-generation college students
- $6.5 million to develop high-quality coursework for use by preschool teachers
- $1 million to study better treatments for enteric diseases and diarrhea in developing countries
- $1.6 million to improve animal health and improve access to veterinary services
- $300,000 for a project to combat family homelessness

Philanthropic organizations, like the Gates Foundation, play a vital role in the United States, and that is why it is important that their leadership be included in this study. Because of limited public dollars as well as the partisanship of American politics, it is often difficult for government and public agencies to reach consensus on how to provide and pay for the services a community may need. Foundations serve to bridge the gap between a community's needs and a government's means. They manage to circumvent the hard obstacles of political rhetoric and governmental restraint to achieve their desired social impact.

Foundations offer a safe and respected space for individuals with different political loyalties to step forward and accomplish what they might otherwise resist in the governmental realm. Their financial support is used to build libraries, hospitals, and playgrounds. They enable improved literacy, promote better child welfare, and provide preventive health care. They support the arts, environmental conservation, and historical preservation. They buy toys for kids, fund scholarships for college students, give clothes to the poor, and find housing for the homeless.

Foundation support also plays an increasingly important role in advancing scientific discoveries. Although foundation dollars constitute only a small fraction of the amount that federal agencies spend on sponsored research, private donors are often willing to support novel studies or new lines of research that the federal government avoids because they are seen as too risky or obscure. Young scientific investigators are particularly likely to benefit from private foundation investments.

The fifty foundations whose leadership is the subject of this chapter can be grouped into three categories:

- The vast majority are *independent* or *private foundations*. Like the Gates Foundation, their funds come primarily from a one-time gift or repeated donations by an individual, a family, or a business. In turn, the foundation awards grants to recipients it believes will further its mission. To be eligible to be classified by the IRS as a private foundation, the entity must pay out at least 5 percent of its assets annually.

  Some independent foundations focus on one type of charitable giving. For example, the Robert Wood Johnson Foundation and the California Endowment support research and programs that advance health. The Duke Endowment, on the other hand, funds a variety of programs, but all of them are for the benefit of people living in North Carolina and South Carolina. The Simons Foundation, in New York City, focuses exclusively on research grants in mathematics and the basic sciences.

  Most private foundations award grants to fund more than one priority area. Gates is a prime example, of course, but so are many others like the Ford Foundation (challenging inequality through projects that reduce poverty, advance human knowledge, and promote democracy), the Charles Steward Mott Foundation (with priorities on education, the environment, civil society on an international scale, and its hometown community of Flint, Michigan), and the Conrad Hilton Foundation (whose targets include Catholic causes, children affected by HIV and AIDS, foster youth, homelessness, safe water, substance use prevention, blindness, disaster relief and recovery, hospitality workforce, and multiple sclerosis).

- Six of the foundations are designated as *community foundations.* Examples are the Tulsa Community Foundation, the Silicon Valley Community Foundation, and the New York City Community Trust. Community foundations are often thought of as public foundations because they solicit and receive funds from a variety of donors—not just a specific individual or family. These donations are combined into one overall endowment. Grants from the endowment's earnings are then distributed, typically on a competitive or formula basis, to advance the quality of life and social benefits of a community or region.
- Three of the foundations are classified as *operating foundations*, meaning they dedicate almost all of their expenditures to the support of a specific program or activity that the foundation manages. For example, the J. Paul Getty Trust primarily supports the operation of the J. Paul Getty Museum. Likewise, the Kimbell Art Foundation was created to build and run the Kimbell Art Museum in Fort Worth, Texas. The Casey Family Programs is an operating foundation that supports its own child welfare programs and policy studies across the nation.

Foundations are meaningful both to the people who give to them and the individuals who are their recipients. In 2015, the more than 100,000 foundations in the United States gave away about $58 billion dollars. The impact of their gifts on a national and even international scale ripples through society on multiple levels, reducing generational poverty, improving public health, cultivating new talent, building community capacity, and enriching cultural literacy. Because of foundations' essential role in supporting the public good, exploring the education of their leadership is every bit as important as our review of elected leaders, big business executives, media chiefs, university leaders, and the military's top brass.

EDUCATIONAL HISTORY

All of the foundation CEOs in this sample earned a college degree. (Risa Lavizzo-Mourey, who headed the Robert Wood Johnson Foundation at the time this book was started, enrolled in medical school at Harvard after completing her junior year at the State University of New York at Stony Brook; even with this early exit from college, she was counted as a graduate, given that she earned her MD at Harvard as well as an MBA from the University of Pennsylvania.)

Forty-three of the foundation CEOs earned a postgraduate degree of some kind, second only to university and college presidents. Seventeen were awarded more than one advanced degree.

Table 4.1 presents the CEOs and their degrees.

UNDERGRADUATE STUDIES

Two-thirds (thirty-seven) of these CEOs attended a private college for their undergraduate education. This is the largest percentage of private institution attendance for any of the seven CEO groups, and it is one of the characteristics that sets the education of this group apart.

Where They Studied

Our foundation sample is one of only two CEO groups where a sizable number—twenty-three to be exact—graduated from one of what was designated in this study as the top-ranked institutions. The other group is the presidents and chancellors of the elite institutions themselves, the topic of chapter 7.

Stanford led the list with four graduates, followed by Harvard (three), and the University of Pennsylvania and Notre Dame with two graduates each. A total of nine foundation CEOs graduated from an Ivy League institution, second only to the university presidents and chancellors.

The extent to which highly selective institutions predominate among this group of executives is even greater if we consider graduates from institutions that were not classified in the top fifty-three, but are very highly esteemed nonetheless. For example, the University of Toronto, from which Stephanie Cuskley (president of the Helmsley Charitable Trust) graduated, is generally regarded as one of the world's twenty best universities. Because it is not located in the United States, it is excluded from the list of national elites.

Add in several liberal arts colleges that missed making the top-ranked list but are always highly rated nationally by the various rating systems—Colgate (alma mater for Lorie Slutsky of the New York Community Trust), Wesleyan (where Knight Foundation CEO Alberto Ibarguen and the Cleveland Foundation's Ronald Richard both graduated), Franklin and Marshall (with graduate Patti Harris at Bloomberg Philanthropies), and Occidental College (Christopher Oechsli with the Atlantic Philanthropies)—and almost 60 percent of the CEOs for America's largest foundations graduated from institutions that enjoy considerable national or international prestige.

Table 4.1 Foundation Heads' Education

CEO	Foundation	Undergraduate Degree	Graduate Degree
Susan Desmond-Hellmann	Bill & Melinda Gates F.	BS Premed U. Nevada	Masters Public Health U. California (Berkeley) MD U. Nevada
Darren Walker	Ford F.	BA Government & BS Speech Communication U. Texas	JD U. Texas
James B. Cuno	J. Paul Getty Trust	BA History Willamette U.	MA History of Art U. Oregon MA & PhD History of Art Harvard
Risa Lavizzo-Mourey	Robert Wood Johnson F.	Attended SUNY (Stony Brook)	MBA U. Pennsylvania MD Harvard
N. Clay Robbins	Lilly Endowment	BA Religion Wabash College	JD Vanderbilt
Larry Kramer	William & Flora Hewlett F.	BA Psychology & Religious Studies Brown	JD U. Chicago
La June Montgomery Tabron	W.K. Kellog F.	BA Business Admin. U. Michigan	MBA Northwestern
Carol S. Larson	David & Lucile Packard F.	BA Stanford	JD Yale
Harvey V. Fineberg	Gordon & Betty Moore F.	BA Psychology Harvard	Masters Public Policy, MD, & PhD Government Harvard
Patricia Harris	Bloomberg Philanthropies	BA Government Franklin & Marshall College	
Emmett D. Carson	Silicon Valley Community F.	BA Economics Morehouse College	MA & PhD Public & International Affairs Princeton
Julia Stasch	John D. & Catherine T. MacArthur F.	BA American History Loyola U. (Chicago)	MA Teaching American History U. Illinois (Chicago)
Earl Lewis	Andrew W. Mellon F.	BA History & Psychology Concordia College	PhD History U. Minnesota
Stephanie Cuskley	Leona M. & Harry B. Helmsley Charitable Trust	BA Economics & Commerce U. Toronto	MBA Cornell
F. Christopher Stone	Open Society F.	BA Social Studies Harvard	MPhil Criminology Cambridge JD Yale
Judith Rodin	Rockefeller F.	BA Psychology U. Pennsylvania	PhD Psychology Columbia
Phil Lakin Jr.	Tulsa Community F.	BA Economics & Finance Baylor U.	MBA Baylor U.

(Continued)

Table 4.1 (*Continued*)

CEO	Foundation	Undergraduate Degree	Graduate Degree
Robert K. Ross	The California Endowment	BA U. Pennsylvania	MPA & MD U. Pennsylvania
Rip Rapson	Kresge F.	BA Political Science Pomona College	JD Columbia
Rhett N. Mabry	Duke Endowment	BA History & Economics U. North Carolina	MHA Duke
Vartan Gregorian	Carnegie Corporation of New York	BA History Stanford	PhD History & Humanities Stanford
Heather Templeton Dill	John Templeton F.	BA History Notre Dame	MA American History Villanova U.
P. Russell Hardin	Robert W. Woodruff F.	BA U. Virginia	JD Duke
Barbara Picower	JPB F.	BA Political Science Hofstra U.	MA History & Secondary Education MS Nutrition New York U.
Allen Greenberg	Susan Thompson Buffett F.	BA SUNY (Buffalo)	JD New York U.
Christine M. Morse	Margaret A. Cargill Philanthropies	BA Accounting Gustavus Adolphus College	
Patrick McCarthy	Annie E. Casey F.	BA Psychology Manhattan College	MA Social Work U. Pennsylvania PhD Social Work Bryn Mawr College
Ridgway H. White	Charles Stewart Mott F.	BA Architecture, Economics & Urban Planning Hobart College	
Kyle Peterson	Walton Family F.	BA International Studies American U.	MBA & MPA U. Texas
Peter Laugharn	Conrad N. Hilton F.	BA American Studies Stanford	MA American Studies Georgetown U. PhD Education U. London
Lorie A. Slutsky	New York Community Trust	BA Colgate U.	MA New School for Social Research
Shelby M.C. Davis	Shelby Cullom Davis Charitable fund	BA History Princeton	
Deborah Wilkerson	Greater Kansas City Community F.	BA Psychology U. Kansas	JD U. Kansas
Eric M. Lee	Kimbell Art F.	BA Art History Yale	
Seward Prosser Mellon	Richard King Mellon F.	BA English Susquehanna U.	MA & PhD Art History Yale

Name	Foundation	Undergraduate	Graduate
Marilyn H. Simons	Simons F.	BA Economics SUNY (Stony Brook)	PhD Economics SUNY (Stony Brook)
Laura Sparks	William Penn F.	BA Philosophy Wellesley College	MBA & JD U. Pennsylvania
Sanford R. Cardin	Charles & Lynn Schusterman Family F.	BA Harvard	JD U. Maryland
Terry Mazany	Chicago Community Trust	BA Anthropology U. Arizona	MA Anthropology & MBA U. Arizona MA Education Policy U. Illinois (Chicago)
Alberto Ibarguen	John S. & James L. Knight F.	BA History Wesleyan U.	JD U. Pennsylvania
Kate Wolford	McKnight F.	BA History Gettysburg College	MA Public Policy & MA Divinity U. Chicago
William C. Bell	Casey Family Programs	BS Biology & Behavioral Sciences Delta State U.	MSW Hunter College PhD Social Welfare City University of New York
Molly McUsic	Wyss F.	BA Economics Notre Dame	JD Harvard
Christopher G. Oechsli	The Atlantic Philanthropies	BA Occidental College	MA Foreign Affairs & JD U. Virginia
Ronald B. Richard	Cleveland F.	BA History Wesleyan U.	MA International Relations Johns Hopkins U.
Wendy Guillies	Ewing Marion Kauffman F.	BA Journalism U. Nebraska	
Rachel Garbow Monroe	Harry & Jeanette Weinberg F.	BA Urban Studies & Art History Northwestern	MBA Northwestern
Don Howard	James Irvine F.	BS Industrial Eng. Stanford	MBA Stanford
Gerun Riley	Eli & Edythe Broad F.	BS Neuroscience Bowdoin College	
Paul L. Joskow	Alfred P. Sloan F.	BA Economics Cornell	PhD Economics Yale

What They Studied

Social studies and humanities were the most numerous undergraduate majors for this group, each accounting for about a third of the undergraduate fields of study. The most popular specific majors were history, economics, or a dual major involving economics and psychology, in that order. Fewer than 10 percent of foundation CEOs majored in a STEM field. Only two of them had a business major. In fact, other than military officers, this group of CEOs was the least likely to have graduated with an undergraduate business degree.

GRADUATE STUDIES

Of the forty-three foundation CEOs earning at least one graduate degree, thirty-one, or 72 percent, earned their highest degree from a private institution, a slightly higher percentage than at the undergraduate level. As was the case with their undergraduate degrees, a very significant number—twenty-nine (or 67 percent)—of these CEOs received their most advanced degrees from top-ranked institutions, second again only to the university presidents and chancellors.

Where They Studied

Harvard and Yale each granted four graduate degrees, followed by the University of Pennsylvania, which granted three degrees, and six others awarding two apiece—Stanford, Duke, Columbia, Northwestern, the University of Chicago, and the University of Texas. Six other top-ranked institutions had one graduate each—Cornell, Vanderbilt, Princeton, Johns Hopkins, the University of Virginia, and the University of Maryland. Fifteen of the foundation heads' graduate/professional degrees were awarded by an Ivy League school.

What They Studied

The JD was the most common advanced degree, earned by fourteen of the foundation heads. The PhD was second, conferred on eleven individuals, followed by a master's degree in varied disciplines (seven), the MBA (five) and the MD (three). Two individuals earned MBA degrees along with master's degrees, and one foundation head (Harvey Fineberg) earned an MD and a PhD.

As was the case with their undergraduate majors, foundation CEOs most often completed their master's and PhD studies in either a social science or a discipline within the humanities. Such specializations tended to align well with the various missions of the foundations that the CEOs subsequently directed.

Whether measured by the percentage of individuals who hold advanced degrees or who attended highly prestigious institutions, foundation chief executives are a very highly educated group of individuals. Their profiles exceed those of any other CEO group except for the higher education leaders. In fact, the educational backgrounds of these two types of leaders bear remarkable similarities to each other.

There is a straightforward explanation for why the education of foundation leaders resembles that of university leaders: foundation CEOs have frequently pursued successful careers in both settings. Among these foundation CEOs, more than 30 percent had held a faculty position, been a college department head or college dean, or served as president of an institution prior to assuming their current foundation role. In many instances, their academic careers have played out, just like their own educational backgrounds, at some of the nation's most highly prestigious universities.

A number of foundation heads came to their posts from the ranks of the faculty or university research centers, sometimes with an initial or intervening stop in government or at an organization with a mission related to the work they would ultimately undertake at the foundation.

- Wyss Foundation CEO Molly McUsic earned tenure on the law faculty at the University of North Carolina, where she specialized in property law and natural resources law. After a stint as an attorney for Secretary of the Interior Bruce Babbit during the Clinton administration, she moved to the top spot at Wyss.
- James Cuno, chief executive for the Getty Trust, held faculty positions at three internationally acclaimed institutions—Vassar, Harvard, and the University of London. Author of several critically praised books on museums and art collections, he also directed art museums at Harvard, London, Dartmouth, and UCLA, before serving a two-year term as the director of the Art Institute of Chicago, widely regarded as one of the world's most influential art museums.
- Rip Rapson, the CEO for the Kresge Foundation, served as deputy mayor of Minneapolis for four years, where he started the Minneapolis Neighborhood Revitalization Project. After an unsuccessful election bid to become mayor of Minneapolis, he was appointed a senior fellow at the University of Minnesota, responsible for overseeing a long-term, multidisciplinary project on the redevelopment of aging suburban communities.
- After graduating from Harvard Medical School and completing her residency at Brigham and Women's Hospital, Risa Lavizzo-Mourey began her academic career as an assistant professor at the University of Pennsylvania. She was eventually named the Sylvan Eisman Professor of Medicine and Health Care Systems and served as director of Penn's Institute on Aging and was chief of geriatric medicine at its medical school.

In 2001 Lavizzo-Mourey became senior vice president of the Robert Wood Johnson Foundation (RWJ), the very organization that had funded her earlier postgraduate research and had kept its eyes on her highly successful career all along the way. Following the retirement of the foundation's prior CEO, Steven Schroeder, Lavizzo-Mourey became president and chief executive officer of the RWJ Foundation in 2003, the first woman to hold the position.

Several other foundation executives ascended the administrative ladders of academia and enjoyed outstanding reputations and distinguished careers as university leaders.

- Larry Kramer was a highly influential legal scholar at a number of universities before becoming CEO of the Hewlett Foundation in 2012. He was on the law faculties of the University of Chicago, University of Michigan, and New York University before being lured west in 2004 to become the Richard E. Lang Professor of Law and dean of the Stanford Law School.

  Kramer's eight years at Stanford were transformational; in the words of one colleague, "He was the dean of yes. If he could possibly say yes, he turned himself inside out, professionally and personally, to make something happen."[2] Kramer was not the first law school dean that Hewlett had recruited. His predecessor, Paul Brest, had also come to Hewlett immediately after completing a term as the dean of the Stanford Law School.
- Harvey V. Fineberg earned his undergraduate degree and three graduate degrees from Harvard University before joining its faculty. After about nine years as a faculty member, he became the dean of Harvard's School of Public Health, a position he held for thirteen years. He then was named provost at Harvard. Fineberg served as president of the prestigious Institute of Medicine from 2002–2014 and then accepted the call to be the chief executive at the Gordon and Betty Moore Foundation.
- After earning his PhD from the University of Minnesota, Mellon Foundation CEO Earl Lewis spent four years as an assistant professor of African American Studies at the University of California Berkeley. He then was recruited to the University of Michigan, where he directed the Center for Afro-American and African Studies and was later appointed dean of Michigan's Graduate School. In 2004 he went to Emory University to become its provost, the position from which he was selected to be Mellon's president in 2012.
- Prior to his appointment at the Carnegie Corporation, Vartan Gregorian taught history as a member of the faculties at San Francisco State College, UCLA, and the University of Texas. He joined the faculty of the University of Pennsylvania in 1972. At Penn, he served as dean of Arts and Sciences and then became the university's twenty-third provost. Gregorian served as president of the New York Public Library from 1981–1989, after which

he was named president of Brown University, a position he held for nine years.

- Before becoming the CEO of the Rockefeller Foundation, Judith Rodin began her academic career as a highly published psychologist on the faculty, first at New York University and then Yale. At Yale, she climbed the ranks from chair of the Department of Psychology, to dean of Arts and Sciences, and eventually to provost. In 1994, she was appointed the seventh president of the University of Pennsylvania, becoming the first woman to head an Ivy League institution. She served ten years in that position, and in 2005 was picked for the top spot at Rockefeller.
- Following a highly successful and lucrative career as a clinical scientist specializing in oncology at Genetech, Susan Desmond-Hellman was picked to be the chancellor at the University of California at San Francisco (UCSF), the same institution where she completed her residency training in the 1980s. The first woman to hold that position, Desmond-Hellman led UCSF from 2009 through 2013, creating a new business model for the one campus in the UC system that is devoted solely to graduate medical education. She took over executive leadership for the Gates Foundation in 2014.

On occasion, the path from academia to foundation leadership has been reversed. After spending four years at the William Penn Foundation, the last two as its CEO, Laura Sparks was appointed president of the Cooper Union for the Advancement of Science and Art in New York City.

What accounts for the substantial overlap between academic careers and foundation leadership? For one thing, university leaders are well known to the trustees of large foundations because they have often spent years cultivating them for gifts on behalf of their campuses, particularly during large capital campaigns. Those relationships obviously serve them well as foundation trustees begin their periodic headhunting for new leadership, on the lookout for that crucial ability of a foundation head to be, in the words of Hewlett Foundation's Fay Twersky, an "artful juggler."[3]

University administrators also are very experienced in managing institutions that possess large resources and serve multiple constituents, two defining qualities of philanthropic organizations. They are comfortable around big money, and they are accustomed to pleading the case that there is never enough of it.

More crucial, however, may be the fact that universities and foundations share common missions. They are both committed to public service and to the creation of knowledge. University administrators are most effective when they enable the faculty to be strong teachers and do important scholarship. Students are the ultimate beneficiaries of such an environment.

A similar kind of facilitation is at the heart of what a strong foundation leader accomplishes—providing the resources that assist an inventor or an artist or a community to make a crucial breakthrough or start a desperately needed program.

Although the path from ivory towers to foundation boardrooms has been well trod by many of this group, a substantial number of foundation heads have followed a second, very different track, moving into their CEO chairs only after working within the organization—often, initially in its back rooms—for many years.

In some instances, they have been members of the family whose wealth created the foundation. Marilyn Simons at the Simons Foundation, Seward Prosser Mellon of the Richard King Mellon Foundation, and Shelby M.C. Davis at the Shelby Cullom Davis Charitable Fund come to mind.

More often, however, they have exemplified the successful homegrown chief executives that Jim Collins lauded in *Good to Great*[4]—leaders who learned the work and values of their foundations from the inside out and established hard-earned trust, knowledge, and credibility from years of well-informed service to the organization.

- Christine Morse joined a management training program at agribusiness giant Cargill in 1977, fresh out of Gustavus Adolphus College with her accounting degree in hand. She worked in several of the company's divisions, took a year off to teach at her alma mater, and ultimately returned to the company and became close to Margaret Cargill, granddaughter and heir to the company's founder W. W. Cargill. Morse has been the only CEO in the history of the Margaret A. Cargill Foundation, which was created at the time of Ms. Cargill's death in 2006.
- La June Montgomery Tabron began working at the W.K. Kellogg Foundation in 1987, starting out as its controller. Across her twenty-six years with the organization, she has held the titles of treasurer, vice president for finance, and executive vice president for operations. Explaining her long-time loyalty to Kellogg, which was rewarded by her being named its CEO in 2013, Tabron said, "I like to abide by the hedgehog principal—keep working hard, keep working forward, always contributing to the success of the team and the organization."[5]
- Wendy Guillies is another "insider" success story. She worked at the Kauffman Foundation for fifteen years before becoming its president in 2015. A graduate of the nearby University of Kansas and a native of Kansas City, where the Kauffman Foundation is headquartered, Guillies worked for the three previous Kauffman CEOs before taking over the job herself.
- With a PhD in social work, Patrick McCarthy established a national reputation as an expert in children and family services. Early in his career, he worked as a psychiatric social worker, taught at a couple of universities, and directed

Delaware's juvenile corrections program. McCarthy first came to the Annie E. Casey Foundation in 1994 to oversee a mental health project serving urban children. He has stayed at Casey ever since, assuming a number of increasingly influential leadership positions before being named its president in 2010.

- Rhett Mabry is another individual who rose through the ranks to become a foundation CEO. Mabry joined the Duke Endowment in 1992 as its associate director of health care. Later, he served as the director of the endowment's child care program before being named vice president in 2009. Mabry was named president in 2016, following in the footsteps of the retiring president, Gene Cochrane, who had also been a longtime Duke employee, having joined the endowment in 1980.
- Gerun Riley started in 2003 at the Edythe and Eli Broad Foundation in an entry-level office manager position. Thirteen years later, having served in the positions of chief of staff, vice president, and senior vice president, she took on the top job at Broad, one of the nation's leading foundations for developing educational leadership and innovation. Commenting on Riley's selection, Mr. and Mrs. Broad stated, "We want our philanthropy to continue after we are gone. For some time, we have looked for someone whom we could trust to work with us in overseeing our philanthropic activities, someone who shares our values and priorities. And the right person has been with us the whole time."[6]

To summarize, the chief executive officers of America's largest foundations are a well-educated group who tend to have followed one of two distinct paths to their current posts. A substantial percentage of them prepared for and succeeded in highly visible academic careers before taking a turn at philanthropic leadership. In several instances, they had been influential leaders at one of the nation's most highly respected universities.

The second group consists of individuals who spent many years at the same foundation and were ultimately promoted from within the ranks to the top spot. In some cases, they were relatives of the donors who began the foundation, but more often, they were longtime insiders who earned the respect and confidence of the foundation originators through their years of loyal, effective service.

If we were to draw the composite profile of foundation chief executives, the following four features would be highlighted:

- At both the undergraduate and graduate level, they attended predominantly private institutions.
- They displayed a relatively equal emphasis on the humanities and social sciences for their undergraduate majors, with much less attention devoted to business degrees and STEM fields.
- They earned a majority of all their degrees—baccalaureate, professional, and doctoral—from the nation's top-ranked colleges and universities, with

a particularly strong representation of Ivy League institutions among their alma maters.

- They showed a preference for the JD followed closely by the PhD for their terminal degrees. The MBA was a distant third, having been earned by less than 20 percent of this group.

The CEOs who are the topic of the next chapter—the nation's highest-ranking military leaders—offer a strong contrast to these educational characteristics. Their education was much more likely to have been technical or scientific in nature. And the majority of them were educated at a handful of public institutions, with missions specifically crafted to prepare leadership for the nation's armed services.

NOTES

1. http://www.gatesfoundation.org/How-We Work/Quick Links/Grants-Database
2. https://law.stanford.edu/stanford-lawyer/articles/farewell-larry-krame/
3. http://www.hewlett.org/foundation-chief-executives-as-artful-jugglers/
4. Jim Collins, *Good to Great: Why Some Companies Make the Leap . . . And Others Don't* (Glasgow: William Collins, 2001).
5. http://www.forbes.com/sites/rahimkanani/2014/03/15/an-interview-with-la-june-montgomery-tabron-of-the-w-k-kellogg-foundation/#58b87aae357b
6. http://www.latimes.com/entertainment/arts/la-et-cm-broad-foundation-president-20160819-snap-story.html

Chapter 5

Military Chief Executives

At the beginning of this project, a list of CEO categories was identified, with the aim of broadly sampling the most influential chief executives across the nation. A wide net was cast that included state and local elected officials, opinion makers in the media, foundation heads, and university presidents, along with the usual Fortune 500 suspects.

This process resulted in six categories that appeared to be comprehensive and that would allow the investigation of more than just the corporate honchos who ran the nation's biggest businesses. The sample included leaders who acted across a broad terrain of American life and who were responsible for our major institutions, not just the companies from which we bought our cars, TVs, and gasoline. The process and the resulting lists looked to be thorough.

Just to be safe, the list was given to a colleague, who was asked one simple question, "Is anyone missing?" He looked it over and paused only briefly before giving a two-word answer: "The military." Of course, he was right. That's why there are now seven categories.

No doubt, President Trump would approve this notion of military leaders as CEOs. He picked three former general officers to serve in his cabinet, including two former four-star generals to head up major executive branch departments—James Mattis at the Department of Defense and John Kelly to be Secretary of Homeland Security.

In this chapter, the education of the forty highest-ranking military leaders in the nation is reviewed. They are the active four-star officers, which includes twenty-nine generals (fourteen in the Air Force, eleven in the Army, and four in the Marines) along with eleven admirals (nine in the Navy and two in the Coast Guard). The only higher rank than that attained by these men and women is a five-star insignia, but it is reserved for senior military commanders operating during wartime and has been worn by only ten men in US history.

Before examining the education of these leaders, which, as we shall see, is the most homogeneous of any of the chief executive groups, it might be helpful to learn a bit more about the institutions that have been established specifically for the purpose of educating military officers in the United States.

MILITARY ACADEMIES AND COLLEGES

The United States maintains several kinds of institutions to train officers for its military. For the purposes of this book, the important ones to consider fall into three categories: the service academies, the senior military colleges, and several institutions that specialize in postgraduate education for military leaders and civilians in defense-related agencies.

Service Academies

The United States operates five service academies charged with the mission of providing an undergraduate education to commissioned officers in our armed services:

- The US Military Academy (USMA) in West Point, New York. Officially founded in 1802 through legislation signed by Thomas Jefferson, West Point's current enrollment is about 4,300 Army cadets.
- The US Naval Academy, in Annapolis, Maryland. The Naval Academy was founded in 1845 as the Naval School through the efforts of then Secretary of Navy George Bancroft. It enrolls about 4,500 midshipmen.
- The US Coast Guard Academy in New London, Connecticut. The Coast Guard Academy was founded in 1876, and its initial instruction was conducted on a two-masted scooner, named the *Dobbin*. Its first land-based campus was at Curtis Bay, Maryland, before it moved to its current location at New London in 1910. The Coast Guard Academy's corps of cadets numbers about 900.
- The US Merchant Marine Academy in Kings Point, New York. Founded when Congress passed the Merchant Marine Act in 1936, the permanent campus was completed and dedicated by President Franklin D. Roosevelt in 1943. The Merchant Marine Academy enrolls approximately 900 midshipmen.

- The US Air Force Academy in Colorado Springs, Colorado. After the Air Force was established as a separate branch of service in 1947, Congress passed a bill that authorized the founding of the academy in 1954. Its enrollment is about 4,100 cadets.

The service academies are highly selective institutions. Applicants are required to be nominated by a member of Congress or, in some selected instances, by the vice president or president (the Coast Guard Academy is an exception; it does not use a nomination process). There are limits on how many nominations a member of Congress can make for a given vacancy as well as on how many cadets per nominator can attend an academy at any one time. Entrance to the Air Force Academy or the Naval Academy also requires a personal interview. The competition for admission among nominees is always fierce, with the average acceptance rate to the academies ranging between 9 and 17 percent.

Once admitted, cadets and midshipmen receive a "full ride" in financial aid. All tuition is paid. Room and board are covered. In addition, cadets and midshipmen receive a monthly stipend. After graduation, service academy graduates are commissioned as officers and must serve a minimum term of duty, typically five years of active-duty plus another three years in the reserves.

The service academies fare extremely well in the college ranking systems. For example, in 2017, *U.S. News and World Report* ranked the Naval Academy twelfth among its national liberal arts colleges, the highest of any public college and tied with the likes of Colby, Colgate, Hamilton, Haverford, Smith, and Vassar. The US Military Academy placed nineteenth on that same list, tied with Grinnell College in Iowa. And the Air Force Academy came in at thirty-second, the same as Bucknell, Holy Cross, and Pitzer.

If one wanted to attribute elite status to these three academies, based on the usual indices that most of the ranking systems employ, it would be hard to argue against it. They are very selective, although it is always wise to remain skeptical about how student selectivity is calculated, even by the service academies. They graduate the vast majority of their students—on time and without college-related debt. A high percentage of their graduates go on to very successful careers, both in the military and in civilian life.

Senior Military Colleges

The senior military colleges (SMCs) combine a college education with military instruction in the form of a reserved officer training corps (ROTC) program that is completed by "cadets." At some SMCs, all the undergraduates are required to be cadets; at others, the cadets make up just a fraction of the overall undergraduate enrollment. They typically live together in on-campus residence halls and wear a distinctive military-style uniform.

Cadets maintain a schedule and live by a set of rules that are similar to those of the service academies. They are free to major in any field they choose. Upon graduation, cadets can be commissioned as officers, but, unlike graduates from the military academies, they are not required to enter military service, unless they received an ROTC scholarship.

- Norwich University. Located in Northfield, Vermont, Norwich University (also known as the Military College of Vermont) is the oldest SMC in the country and is the only one that is private. It is credited with being the birthplace of ROTC and still maintains training in four service branches—Army, Navy, Air Force, and Marines. Of its approximately 2,900 undergraduates, 60 percent are in the Corps of Cadets.
- Texas A&M University in College Station, Texas. Texas A&M is the largest university among the SMCs (with an enrollment of more than 60,000 students) and maintains the largest corps of cadets of all the SMCs, numbering about 2,450 men and women. Participation in the Texas A&M corps was mandatory for many years; it became voluntary in 1965.
- The Citadel. Founded in 1842 and located in Charleston, South Carolina, The Citadel (also known as the Military College of South Carolina) enrolls about 2,300 undergraduates, all of whom are cadets (its civilian students can earn undergraduate and graduate degrees through online and evening programs).
- The University of North Georgia is located in Dahlonega, Georgia. Also known as the Military College of Georgia, it offers only an Army ROTC program to about 750 cadets, who are part of a total undergraduate enrollment of more than 16,000 students.
- Virginia Military Institute. VMI was founded in 1839, making it the oldest public SMC in the country. Located in Lexington, Virginia, its enrollment is about 1,700 cadets, who are required to participate in one of the four ROTC programs.
- Virginia Polytechnic Institute and State University. Virginia Tech, which is located in Blacksburg, Virginia, enrolls about 30,500 students, making it the second largest SMC in overall enrollment. Like Texas A&M, its corps of cadets, which numbers about 1,100, mingles with the much larger civilian student body. Participation in its corps became voluntary in 1964.

UNDERGRADUATE STUDY

Table 5.1 presents the four-star officers and their degrees.

Table 5.1 Four Star Officers' Education

Officer	Branch	Undergraduate Degree	Graduate Degree
Joseph F. Dunford Jr.	Marines	BA Political Science St. Michael's College	MA International Relations Tufts U. MA Government Georgetown U.
Paul J. Selva	Air Force	BS Aeronautical Eng. Air Force Academy	MS Management & Human Relations Abilene Christian U. MS Political Science Auburn U.
Thomas D. Waldhauser	Marines	BA Psychology Bemidji State U.	Master's National Security Strategies National War College
Joseph L. Votel	Army	BS US Military Academy	Graduate of Army War College
Curtis M. Scaparrotti	Army	BS US Military Academy	MA Administrative Education U. South Carolina
Lori J. Robinson	Air Force	BA English U. New Hampshire	MA Education Leadership Troy State U. MA National Security & Strategic Studies Naval War College
Harry B. Harris Jr.	Navy	BS Engineering US Naval Academy	MPA Harvard MA National Security Studies Georgetown U.
Kurt W. Tidd	Navy	BS Foreign Area Studies US Naval Academy	MA Political Science U. Bordeaux
Raymond A. Thomas III	Army	BS US Military Academy	MA International Studies Army War College MS International Studies Naval Command & Staff College
John E. Hyten	Air Force	BS Engineering & Applied Sciences Harvard U.	MBA Auburn U.
Darren W. McDew	Air Force	BS Civil Eng. Virginia Military Institute	MS Aviation Management Embry-Riddle Aeronautical U.
Joseph L. Lengyel	Air Force	BS Chemistry U North Texas.	MBA U. Tennessee
John W. Nicholson Jr.	Army	BS US Military Academy BA History Georgetown	Master's National Security Studies National War College Master of Military Arts & Sciences School of Advanced Military Studies
Vincent K. Brooks	Army	BS US Military Academy	Master of Military Arts & Sciences School of Advanced Military Studies
Michael S. Rogers	Army	BA Business Auburn U.	MS National Security Strategy National War College
Mark A. Milley	Army	BA Political Science Princeton	MA International Relations Columbia MA National Security & Strategic Studies Naval War College
Daniel B. Allyn	Army	BS US Military Academy	MA National Security & Strategic Studies Naval War College

(Continued)

Table 5.1 *(Continued)*

Officer	Branch	Undergraduate Degree	Graduate Degree
Robert B. Abrams	Army	BS US Military Academy	MS Administration Central Michigan U. Master's Strategic Studies Army War College
Gustave F. Perna	Army	BA Business Management U. Maryland	Master's Logistics Management Florida Institute of Technology
Robert B. Brown	Army	BS US Military Academy	Master of Education U. Virginia MS National Security & Strategic Studies National War College
David G. Perkins	Army	BS US Military Academy	MS Mechanical Eng. U. Michigan MA National Security & Strategic Studies Naval War College
Robert B. Neller	Marines	BA History & Speech Comm. U. Virginia	MA Human Resource Management Pepperdine U.
Glenn M. Walters	Marines	BS Electrical Eng. The Citadel	
John M. Richardson	Navy	BS Physics US Naval Academy	MS Engineering/Oceanography/Applied Ocean Science MIT (Woods Hole) MS National Security Strategy National War College
William F. Moran	Navy	BS English US Naval Academy	MA National Security Strategy National War College
James F. Caldwell Jr.	Navy	BS Marine Eng. US Naval Academy	MS Operations Research Naval Postgraduate School
Philip S. Davidson	Navy	BS Physics US Naval Academy	MA National Security & Strategic Studies Naval War College
Michelle J. Howard	Navy	BS US Naval Academy	Master of Military Arts & Sciences Army Command & General Staff College
Scott H. Swift	Navy	BS Industrial Arts San Diego State U.	MA National Security & Strategic Studies Naval War College
David L. Goldfein	Air Force	BS Philosophy Air Force Academy	MBA Oklahoma City U.
Stephen W. Wilson	Air Force	BS Aerospace Eng. Texas A&M U.	MS Engineering Management South Dakota School of Mines MS Strategic Studies Air War College

Herbert J. Carlisle	Air Force	BS Math Air Force Academy	MBA Golden Gate U.
Robin Rand	Air Force	BS Aviation Science Air Force Academy	MS Aeronautical Science Embry-Riddle Aeronautical U. MA National Security & Strategic Studies Naval War College
Ellen M. Pawlikowski	Air Force	BS Chemical Eng. New Jersey Institute of Technology	PhD Chemical Eng. U. California (Berkeley)
John W. Raymond	Air Force	BS Administrative Management Clemson U.	MS Admin. Management Central Michigan U. MA National Security & Strategic Studies Naval War College
Carleton D. Everhart II	Air Force	BS Agriculture Virginia Polytechnic U.	MS Business Management U. Arkansas MA National Security Strategy National War College
Terrence J. O'Shaughnessy	Air Force	BS Aeronautical Eng. Air Force Academy	MS Aeronautical Sciences Embry Riddle Aeronautical U.
Tod D. Wolters	Air Force	BS Air Force Academy	MS Aeronautical Science Technology Embry-Riddle Aeronautical U. MA Strategic Studies Army War College
Paul F. Zukunft	Coast Guard	BS Government Coast Guard Academy	MA Management Webster U. MA National Security & Strategic Studies Naval War College
Charles D. Michel	Coast Guard	BS Marine Eng. Coast Guard Academy	JD U. Miami

Note: General Votel's biographies do not specify the graduate degree earned at the Army War College.

All of the forty four-star officers earned a college degree, which is, in fact, a requirement for military service at this level, and thirty-nine of the forty were awarded at least one graduate degree.

Where They Studied

Among all groups of executives, the active four-star officers graduated from the narrowest set of institutions, with twenty-four (60 percent) of them receiving their degrees from one of the service academies. If we add in the graduates from the SMCs, the number of alumni from institutions that carry some type of military designation grows to twenty-eight (70 percent).

The US Military Academy at West Point led the list with nine graduates, followed by the Naval Academy at Annapolis with seven, the Air Force Academy at Colorado Springs with six, and the Coast Guard Academy in New London with two. The SMCs produced four graduates—one each from Texas A&M, The Citadel, VMI, and Virginia Tech.

A total of twelve officers earned degrees from civilian institutions and were commissioned as officers from an on-campus ROTC program. Nine graduated from a public university, with the University of Virginia and the University of Maryland being the two top-ranked public institutions on the list. Only four officers received an undergraduate degree from a private civilian institution: Harvard, Princeton, and St. Michael's College graduated one officer apiece. General John Nicholson has two undergraduate degrees, one from the US Military Academy and one from Georgetown University.

Although the prototype for the top brass of the military is to attend a service academy or military college, it is obviously not an absolute prerequisite for "four stardom." As the prime example, the current chairman of the Joint Chiefs of Staff, General Joseph Dunford, graduated from St. Michael's College, a small, Catholic liberal arts institution in Colchester, Vermont.

General Dunford, who as chair of the Joint Chiefs is the nation's highest-ranking military officer, also earned two graduate degrees, and neither was from a military institution. Interviewed by the college's alumni magazine about his time at St. Michael's, Dunford said that a Catholic liberal arts education was the perfect preparation for his military career: "Critical thinking and reading skills have been invaluable. It prepared me to properly frame complex issues and challenges. Years of Catholic education also influenced me to seek opportunities to serve others—a critical aspect of leadership."[1]

By the way, Dunford is not the only ROTC graduate to lead the Joint Chiefs. Colin Powell, George W. Bush's secretary of state and probably the best-known chair of the Joint Chiefs in recent years, graduated from City College of New York (CCNY) with a major in geology and a commission from CCNY's Army ROTC program. He later earned an MBA, again from a nonmilitary institution—George Washington University.

Other examples of current military commanders who were commissioned from civilian universities include Robert B. Neller, the commandant of the Marine Corps, who received his undergraduate degree in history and speech communications from the University of Virginia. He followed that up with an MA in human resource management from Pepperdine.

The head of the US Strategic Command (formerly known as the Strategic Air Command), General John E. Hyten, earned both of his degrees from civilian institutions—Harvard for his BS in engineering and applied sciences and Auburn for his MBA.

Ellen Pawlikowski, who is in charge of the Air Force Material Command, entered the military out of the ROTC program at the New Jersey Institute of Technology. She is the only current four-star general who holds a PhD, earned from the University of California (Berkeley) in chemical engineering.

What They Studied

At all colleges and universities, the requirements of the curriculum usually undergo several changes over the years as the faculty engages in ongoing debates about what should constitute a core curriculum, which courses should be required versus serve as electives, and what the minimum number of credits should be for graduation. At the service academies, these changes have been profound.

Take West Point, for example. From its inception in 1802 until 1960, all cadets completed the same courses in a curriculum that was largely focused on engineering. In fact, the US Military Academy is often credited with being the United States' first engineering college. Starting in 1960, elective courses were introduced, and by 1970, cadets could concentrate on certain fields of study in which they developed more depth.[2]

The concept of majors was not introduced until 1985, and completing a major did not become a requirement for graduation until the cadet class of 2005.[3] One result of this curricular history is that several of the officers listed in table 5.1 did not have a declared major upon graduation from one of the service academies.

Currently, West Point cadets are required to complete a total of forty courses for graduation, and twelve of those must be core courses in math, science, and engineering. These thirty-six hours of instruction would be the equivalent to at least a minor in a STEM discipline at most universities.

The emphasis on STEM education is, if anything, even stronger at the Naval Academy and the Air Force Academy. Midshipmen are required to complete fifteen specific STEM courses for graduation, and while they are free to declare a major of their choice, beginning with the class of 2013, 65 percent of the graduates commissioned to be naval officers must have completed a STEM major. At the Air Force Academy, fifteen of the thirty-two required core courses are in the basic sciences, engineering, and an interdisciplinary science and technology course.

Consistent with the strong science and engineering components of their curricula, the five service academies grant the BS degree to all their undergraduates.

For those officers for whom a formal major could be confirmed, the majority were trained in a STEM discipline. Engineering was the most popular major by far, declared by more than a quarter of the graduates.

Even among the officers who graduated from somewhere other than a service academy, science and engineering were the most frequently declared majors. But as already suggested, because of the prominence of STEM courses among the required core, the number of formal STEM majors underestimates the extent to which science and engineering were the predominant concentrations of these officers. No other group of CEOs begins to rival the military officers when it comes to having a sound education in scientific, engineering, and technical fields.

Athletics at the Academies

Intercollegiate athletics plays a significant role in the campus life and institutional profile of almost every college and university in America, but their place in military education—particularly at the service academies—is distinctive and deserves additional attention. In recognition of the physical demands of military service, all the service academies have in place requirements that cadets and midshipmen participate in athletic activities throughout their undergraduate careers, and about 80 percent of the entering students played a varsity sport in high school.

The athletic requirement can be met in various ways, such as participating in club sports or playing on intramural teams. However, intercollegiate athletics are very important at the academies as well. All three of the largest academies—Army, Air Force, and Navy—support NCAA Division I athletics for both men's and women's sports. At the Coast Guard and the Merchant Marine academies, students compete in the NCAA's Division III.

The academies have graduated some outstanding sports stars who, after finishing their military commitment, went on to become very well-known professional athletes. Naval Academy graduate David Robinson was the top pick by the San Antonio Spurs in the 1987 NBA draft and was named Rookie of the Year and league MVP and led the Spurs to two NBA titles. Roger Staubach, another Naval Academy product, won the Heisman Trophy in 1963, and after four years of military service was drafted in the tenth round by the Dallas Cowboys, the team the six-time Pro Bowler subsequently led to two Super Bowl titles. The Air Force's Chad Hennings played for nine years with the Dallas Cowboys, and Billy Hurley, from the Naval Academy, became the first service academy graduate to join the PGA tour, debuting in 2012.

In fact, on-field and on-court athletic competition became important enough to the academies that in 2016 they changed their long-standing policy that required a mandatory twenty-four months of active-duty upon graduation. Under this revised rule, a service academy graduate who wanted to play a pro sport could request an appointment in the reserves upon graduation to satisfy the service obligation. This exemption was short-lived. In 2017, Defense Secretary James Mattis rescinded it and reinstated the requirement that all academy graduates serve at least two years of active-duty following graduation.

Though not as famous as "The Admiral" Robinson or "Roger the Dodger" Staubach, several of the current four-star officers enjoyed outstanding intercollegiate athletic careers at the academies. They followed in the footsteps of the likes of Dwight Eisenhower, who played linebacker and running back for Army, and George Patton, who competed in the modern pentathlon at the 1912 Olympics.

- Harry Harris Jr., commander of the US Pacific Command, was a varsity saber fencer at the Naval Academy. Returning to Annapolis in 2016 for the annual alumni versus varsity fencing meet, Harris claimed, "Fencing instilled in me a sense of focused aggression, not just individually, but as part of a team, something that has been valuable to me throughout my career."[4]
- General Vincent K. Brooks and General Robert B. Brown both played basketball for Army under the legendary coach Mike Krzyzewski, himself a graduate of West Point. Brooks played for a year before giving up basketball to concentrate on his studies. He subsequently became the first African American in the history of the US Military Academy to hold the prestigious post of captain of cadets, often referred to as First Captain.
- Bob Brown turned down a scholarship to play basketball at the University of Michigan and took to the court for the Black Knights instead, even wearing Brooks's old number forty-four. Brown was a prolific scorer at Army and considered an NBA career before suffering a serious knee injury. He said that he learned more about leadership on the basketball court at West Point than anywhere else.
- At the Air Force Academy, Tod Wolters was a three-year football letterman for the Falcons, playing cornerback in the 1979 season, running back in 1980, and linebacker in 1981. He now is the commander of the US Air Force in Europe and Africa and also serves as commander of Allied Air Command.

- Terrence O'Shaughnessy, was another three-year Falcon letterman as a hockey player. President Barack Obama appointed him to be commander of the Pacific Air Forces.

GRADUATE STUDIES

All but one of the four-star officers earned a postgraduate degree, and seventeen officers (43 percent) earned more than one. This record is not surprising because a postgraduate degree is expected of officers prior to promotion to the rank of lieutenant colonel or commander.

So necessary is advanced education to the US military that the federal government has established a number of graduate schools for the training of its officers in those fields that are most essential to their missions. For example, the Uniformed Services University of the Health Sciences, located at Fort Sam Houston in Texas, trains doctors, dentists, nurses, and other health care providers for the military.

More important for the four-star officers are the specialized US Department of Defense Senior Service Colleges that offer master's degrees in several concentrations, such as strategic studies and national security. Usually these institutions enroll both senior military officers and civilians from agencies like the State Department or the Department of Defense. Occasionally, military leaders from other countries are accepted into these programs as well. Among the largest and most influential of these institutions are:

- Army War College in Carlisle, Pennsylvania. Founded in 1901, it enrolls about 800 students and counts among its alumni such well-known generals as Dwight Eisenhower, Omar Bradley, Alexander Haig, Tommy Franks, and Norman Schwarzkopf.
- Naval War College in Newport, Rhode Island. This college was established in 1884, making it the oldest of these institutions. Among its distinguished graduates are Astronaut Alan Shepard, Admirals Chester Nimitz and Elmo Zumwalt, and General Stanley McChrystal.
- Air War College at Maxwell Air Force Base in Montgomery, Alabama. One of the newer of the advanced colleges, it was founded in 1946. It counts among its graduates test pilot Chuck Yeager, astronaut Alvin Drew, and US Representative Martha McSally, the first woman to fly in combat for the United States.
- National Defense University (NDU) at Fort Lesley McNair in Washington DC. Congress created the National Defense University in 1976 to bring together several training and education programs designed to prepare military leaders and selected civilians in national security strategy, conduct

military-related research, and integrate technology most effectively into military strategy.

NDU is an accredited university and contains several colleges and centers, including the National War College and the Dwight D. Eisenhower School for National Security and Resource Strategy. Both of these components have been approved to offer master of science degrees.

Where They Studied

As was the case with their undergraduate degrees, most of the four-star officers earned at least one of their graduate degrees from one of the military's specialized training institutions, such as the National War College, the Army War College, and the Naval War College. Twenty-six of the forty four-star officers (65 percent) obtained a graduate degree from one of these institutions or an independent institution with a mission that is closely linked to the military, such as the Embry-Riddle Aeronautical University.

Twenty-three (58 percent) officers also earned at least one advanced degree from a traditional civilian university. All of these were master's degrees with the exception of a PhD in chemical engineering awarded by the University of California (Berkeley) to Air Force general Ellen Pawlikowski and a JD awarded by Miami University to Coast Guard admiral Charles Michel. The only officer to obtain a graduate degree outside of the United States was Admiral Kurt W. Tidd, who was awarded an MA in political science from the University of Bordeaux in France.

Top-ranked universities were modestly represented among the graduate schools attended by the military officers. Eight graduate degrees were awarded by seven top-ranked universities. Georgetown University awarded two graduate degrees. Two Ivy League institutions—Harvard and Columbia—awarded one master's degree each, as did MIT, the University of Virginia, and the University of Michigan. The University of California at Berkeley awarded the one doctoral degree earned by a general.

What They Studied

The most common graduate specialization was a master's degree in security and strategic studies, national security strategy, or military arts and sciences. Several officers completed a degree in a course of study that was somewhat related to military strategy or operations, albeit at a civilian school. Examples of these degrees include an MA in international relations, a master's of logistics management, and an MS in administration or management. Master's-level engineering or science degrees were awarded to six officers, all of them from civilian universities.

Only four officers earned the MBA, and as previously mentioned there were only one PhD and one JD among this group.

Four-star military officers share a remarkably common educational background. The extent to which this is the case is confirmed by several key facts:

- Only six of these forty individuals did not earn at least one of their degrees from a service academy, senior military college, or postgraduate senior service college.
- The basic undergraduate education of the majority of the nation's top military officers is strongly grounded in science, engineering, and technology.
- The most common educational trajectory for four-star officers is to first obtain an undergraduate engineering degree, which is then followed with a graduate degree in strategic, security, or military studies.

Is this scholastic hegemony an advantage or a liability? Does it reflect excessive educational inbreeding? Or does it exemplify maximally relevant career preparation? Does it equip our military leaders with blinders or fit them with lenses?

Service academy critics, like William Astore, who taught history at the Air Force Academy for several years, argue that the academies emphasize STEM subjects to the neglect of the humanities and social sciences. The result is a reductive, number-crunching, overly technological education that Astore believes produces young officers who are "too number-oriented, too rule-bound, too risk-adverse. US military officers, old as well as young, tend to think geopolitical problems—even in destabilized cauldrons like Iraq and Afghanistan—are solvable if you identify and manipulate the right variables. They think history and politics, human and cultural factors, can be controlled or compensated for."[5]

Other critics of the academies raise the more fundamental concern that they are too expensive to operate and no longer that essential to the modern military, amounting to what Army veteran Scott Beauchamp castigated as "bloated government money-sucks that consistently underperform. They are indulgences that taxpayers, who fund them, can no longer afford. They've outlived their use, and it's time to shut them down."[6] Bruce Fleming, a longtime English professor at the Naval Academy, is no less colorful, lambasting the service academies as "military Disneylands for tourists" and "poster boys of the out-of-control entitlement programs that Republicans say they hate."[7]

Overheated rhetoric aside, the academies produce less than 20 percent of the officers now entering the military, and they are whoppingly more expensive than the ROTC programs at civilian universities from which most officers are commissioned.

The estimated cost for graduating a cadet from West Point is in the $300,000 to $400,000 range, and the Air Force Academy lists its total cost per graduate at more than $500,000. These price tags are four times greater than what an ROTC graduate would cost at most universities.

For their part, academy leaders claim that their institutions have evolved substantially in recent years and are increasingly graduating officers who have acquired a genuine understanding of social dynamics and cultural factors. Lt. General Michelle Johnson, who graduated from the Air Force Academy and is now its superintendent, says, "We want people to think critically. I find myself being a champion of the humanities."[8]

Brigadier General Timothy Trainor, who is the academic dean at West Point, explains the expanding importance of the liberal arts for military officers this way, "It's important to develop in young people the ability to think broadly, to operate in the context of other societies and become agile and adaptive thinkers. What you're trying to do is teach them to deal with complexity, diversity, and change. They're having to deal with people from other cultures. They have to think very intuitively to solve problems on the ground."[9]

Aside from the obligated physical education training and the greater number of required math and science courses, the overall curriculum at the service academies—especially at the big three—is not that different from what students encounter at most four-year institutions.

Generally, the academies do offer a smaller menu of majors than most universities and colleges, but regardless of their majors, cadets and midshipmen are required to take courses in history, literature, philosophy, social sciences, and leadership. A foreign language is required for graduation from the Air Force Academy and West Point, and the Naval Academy requires a foreign language for some majors.

If there is a unique narrowness to a service academy education it is to be found not as much in the curriculum as in the demographics and backgrounds of the students themselves. In general, students at the service academies are more similar to one another, and they look more alike and may think more similarly than is the case at civilian universities.

Thanks to aggressive efforts to diversify the profile of cadets and midshipmen, women and nonwhites make up an increasing percentage of the entering classes at the academies, but they still lag national averages by large margins. For example,

- Of the 20.5 million students enrolled in America's colleges and universities, about 57 percent are women. Compare that to the percentages of women at the academies: US Military Academy (17 percent), Naval Academy (23 percent), and Air Force Academy (22 percent).

- Nationwide, about 14.5 percent of college students are black, and 16.5 percent are Hispanic. At the academies, the percentage of black students ranges from a low of 5.9 percent (Air Force) to a high of 9 percent (West Point), and the percentage of Hispanics varies between 10 and 12 percent across the academies.
- Most students enter the service academies right out of high school, and they must not be older than twenty-three at the time they begin. By contrast, presently about 40 percent of college students nationwide are twenty-five years or older.
- Engineering is still the most popular major at the academies, while at most universities, students are more evenly distributed among business, social science, education, and humanities degrees.
- Finally, almost all academy graduates are headed toward the same career field at least for the first five years after they finish their degrees, while students at civilian colleges are preparing for a much fuller spectrum of occupational pursuits.

Whether there is too much sameness in the educational backgrounds of our top military leaders or whether their training is a model of well-focused relevance will be an ongoing debate, just as there will continue to be the occasional proposals to abolish the service academies and rely on ROTC programs that are cheaper and appear to turn out officers that are every bit as successful in the military as their academy counterparts.

What is certain is that the nation's leading generals and admirals have a unique educational profile among CEOs. They have received extensive higher education concentrated in the applied sciences and technology at the undergraduate level and in security/strategic studies as postgraduates. They also have graduated from a smaller cluster of mostly public, military-mission institutions than those attended by other CEOs.

The merits and the limits of their education profiles are important topics worthy of thoughtful, continuing discussion, and the need for that discussion is a main reason why these military leaders were included in the book.

NOTES

1. http://www.smcvt.edu/pages/get-to-know-us/alumni/dunford-joseph.aspx
2. https://www.aacu.org/publications-research/periodicals/transformation-west-point-liberal-arts-college
3. Ibid.
4. http://usnatrident.blogspot.com/2016/02/usna-fencing-team-takes-on-alumni.html

5. https://contraryperspective.com/2014/12/17/americas-military-academies-are-seriously-flawed/

6. https://www.washingtonpost.com/opinions/why-we-dont-need-west-point/2015/01/23/fa1e1488-a1ef-11e4-9f89-561284a573f8_story.html?utm_term=.3b68143d704a

7. http://www.salon.com/2015/01/05/lets_abolish_west_point_military_academies_serve_no_one_squander_millions_of_tax_dollars/

8. https://www.washingtonpost.com/news/grade-point/wp/2016/04/26/service-academies-where-the-u-s-military-meets-liberal-arts/?utm_term=.bf33b933731e

9. http://www.theatlantic.com/education/archive/2015/10/the-unexpected-schools-championing-the-liberal-arts/410500/

Chapter 6

Media Executives

In this chapter, the education of leading media executives, including the publishers of America's forty most widely read newspapers and the CEOs of ten major network and cable news channels is reviewed. These two groups are interesting for several reasons, not the least of which are the rapidly changing business environment in which newspapers and television news companies must compete and the enormous influence these outlets have on American public opinion.

According to a 2016 report from the Pew Research Center, nearly twice as many adults (38 percent) typically get their news online than obtain it through print (20 percent).[1] The preference for digital news is particularly pronounced for younger adults, while older folks rely most often on the TV for their news. Print newspapers are still read by older Americans, but the traditional fold-and-turn newspapers are seldom read anymore by individuals under forty years of age. The most rapidly growing device for accessing news has become the cell phone, with almost three-quarters of Americans indicating that they read or watch the news at least occasionally on a phone held in the palm of their hands.

Social media, such as Facebook, Twitter, Instagram, and You Tube, have also now become a common source of the news, with 62 percent of US adults receiving at least some of their news through a social media platform.[2] Receiving the news electronically is cheaper, more convenient, and takes advantage of the fact that the majority of US adults now own a cell phone. Despite using digital and social media more and more often, most Americans trust the news information they obtain from those sources much less than that reported in traditional local or national news organizations.

The latest technological innovations—especially the Internet—have transformed journalism just as developments like the printing press, the radio, and the television did in earlier times. And as the very nature of journalism has changed, so too has the way society engages with the news. Bloggers are easily and increasingly mistaken for reporters. Reporters are often replaced by news "aggregators." In-depth stories are giving way to tweets and snapchats. The hoaxes and lies that constitute "fake news" are accorded at least initial credibility by a surprising number of gullible or agenda-driven consumers.

Ever since the Great Recession, these and other changes have led to dire predictions that the traditional newspaper was in a steep decline and would eventually die off. And there is plenty of evidence that the newspaper industry has fallen on hard times unlike anything it has ever seen before. Venerable dailies like the *Cincinnati Post*, the *Rocky Mountain News*, the *Tampa Tribune,* and the *Honolulu Advertiser* have shuttered their doors over the past decade, and almost every newspaper in the country has downsized its workforce in an effort to remain afloat financially.

Advertising revenue continues its downward slide as do newspaper sales and subscriptions. For example, in 2015, overall daily circulation declined by 7 percent from the prior year.[3] Reporters, editors, and photographers are being furloughed, fired, or forced into retirement in growing numbers. In 2015, the newspaper workforce was estimated to be 20,000 positions smaller than it was twenty years earlier.[4]

It's even getting harder and harder to find one of those formerly ubiquitous newspaper boxes on the street corner, where you could drop in your quarters and buy a copy of the paper on the way to work. They have gone the way of the coin-operated pay phone.

Pundits point to a similar fate for cable and TV news, even though both cable and network TV have continued to see small annual revenue increases in recent years. The handwriting does seem to be on the wall for television news as similar threats to what the newspaper industry has already faced are also emerging for the TV news business.

Despite the doom-and-gloom projections, the newspaper industry is managing to hang on, and the TV news business is strategizing with some success to meet its audience challenges. For their part, newspapers have responded to the digital age with several adaptations. Obviously, they have increased their digital circulation, not enough to offset the big drop-off in print-edition readers, but it has helped lessen the overall circulation loss.

Spending on digital advertising has increased, but many web users find the pop-up and pull-down ads more annoying than the old-fashioned ones that stay put in their place on a page, so print advertising persists and for some merchandise, even prevails. Newspapers have also tried to improve their bottom line by diversifying their products with specialty magazines, videography, and other niche publications at the same time that they have consolidated operations by buying up competitors.

One of the lingering and perhaps lasting appeals of an old-fashioned print newspaper is that it publishes the records and documents the local happenings that still matter to people—who got recently arrested, just married, and finally divorced; who graduated with honors; who scored the winning run for the local high school; who bought whose house; and who died. And mundane as it may sound, newspapers still are the primary source to which people turn when they look for the best deals on a car and the biggest sales at the grocery store.

Newspapers also remain important because they continue to employ people who know how to research the facts and write a readable story. They muster content, something that the technology companies don't spend much time or money on. An audience of serious readers remains in America, and while it may be diminishing over time, there are still millions of folks who will spend their money to subscribe to a newspaper so they can read good writing by well-trained journalists.

One other indicator of the continuing relevance of newspapers is how often major chains continue to take them over. Fewer and fewer papers are independently owned as media companies, like Gannett, the Tribune Publishing Company, Hearst, McClatchy, Lee, Advance Publications, and A. H. Belo gobble them up and place them under a bigger umbrella. In 2015 alone, seventy daily newspapers were sold—mostly to larger media companies—for a combined $827 million.[5]

The point is that the newspaper market may be getting smaller, but it remains big enough that major companies believe they can still make money publishing papers. Through mergers and other kinds of restructuring they are giving themselves some additional time and leeway to experiment with new revenue sources and a repositioning of their news strategy. And it just may be working.

After Amazon founder and CEO Jeff Bezos bought the *Washington Post* for $250 million in 2013, he invested another $50 million in its news operations. By the end of 2016, the *Post* announced a 50 percent increase in its online traffic and 75 percent growth in subscriptions during the year, leading to plans to add more than sixty journalists to its staff in 2017.[6] At the same time, the *New York Times*, *Wall Street Journal*, and *Los Angeles Times* were all reporting record increases in their subscriptions.

With respect to television news, viewership of the evening newscasts by ABC, CBS, and NBC increased for three consecutive years, 2013 through 2015. Advertising revenue has followed suit, up substantially during that period. It's much the same story with the cable channels. The cumulative viewership for CNN, Fox News, and MSNBC grew by 8 percent in 2015, fueled largely by a 38 percent increase at CNN.[7]

All this adds up to the fact that newspapers and national television news—the major vehicles of American journalism—continue to matter in the United States. They still are turning profits. They remain trusted sources of information. They agitate millions of people who disagree with their perspectives. They hold public officials more accountable than they would be without them. And through the good writers they still employ, they bring both near and distant events to life, describing them in ways both vivid and true.

Let's now examine the educational histories of the men and women who run these enterprises—the publishers of our largest newspapers and the presidents of the major network and cable news organizations.

NEWSPAPER PUBLISHERS

A newspaper publisher is in charge of the day-to-day operations of the paper. Publishers hire and fire personnel, manage the budget, try to boost sales and other revenue, and oversee the various departments within the operation such as news, advertising, administration, the legal department, and production. Like other CEOs, publishers also are responsible for the figurehead functions of speaking officially on behalf of the paper, representing it in the community, and maintaining good public relations.

As the newspaper business tries to keep pace with the digital revolution and continues to undergo the simultaneous processes of consolidating its ownership and diversifying its products, the traditional notion of a publisher whose sole responsibility is to run a newspaper is giving way to executives who are in charge of media companies that are the parents of subsidiary operations like newspapers, websites, local television stations, cable outlets, business journals, magazines, and a variety of online offerings. Consequently, the official title of publisher is being gradually replaced with the more generic terms such as president or CEO.

Another development as newspapers struggle for their financial lives is to combine the titles (and many of the duties) of publisher and editor. Major papers like the *Chicago Tribune*, the *Chicago Sun Times*, and the *Los Angeles Times* have merged the two roles, melding the business responsibilities of the publisher with the editor's job of overseeing the content and the operations of the newsroom.

These changes suggest that the old red line drawn to protect the integrity of news stories from any undue influence from advertising dollars is being smudged, if not erased, in favor of the bottom line. How such compound positions will work out in the long run is an open question, but this "Doublemint" model may become more common in the future as media companies look for every cost-cutting maneuver possible.

Undergraduate Studies

All but four of the newspaper publishers earned an undergraduate degree, and fifteen of the forty-one earned a graduate degree. (There were forty-one, rather than forty, executives because at the time of this book's writing, Ed Bushey and Debby Krenke were splitting the CEO duties at *Newsday*, following the resignation of Gordon McLeod.) Although this is a high level of degree completion, the percentages of both baccalaureate and graduate degree holders are the lowest of any of our executive groups. Table 6.1 summarizes the degrees for the publishers.

Where They Studied

Newspaper publishers were more likely to have earned their undergraduate degrees at a public college or university than at a private institution. Only nine of their thirty-seven degrees (less than 25 percent) were earned at one of the top-ranked universities, and the only one of those institutions to have granted more than one degree to these executives was the University of Illinois, with two. The other top-ranked institutions were Harvard, Yale, Brown, Stanford, Northwestern, the University of Chicago, and the University of Maryland.

Newspaper publishers tend most to resemble governors and big-city mayors in their pattern of college attendance. They often stayed close to home, enrolling in institutions in the city where they grew up or attending in-state schools where they could take advantage of the subsidized tuition offered to residents. They also frequently worked at part-time jobs for local media outlets while they were going to school. As examples:

- Cheryl Dell grew up in Modesto, California, about an hour and a half south of Sacramento. In high school, she worked as an intern at a local radio station, and even hosted her own show. "It was one of those Sunday morning talk shows that nobody listened to, but the FCC required it," she recalls.[8] After high school, she attended Modesto Community College and then enrolled at California State University, Sacramento, primarily because of its affordability but also because having decided to be a communications major, she was enamored with the city's extensive media opportunities— TV stations affiliated with all three major networks, two newspapers, and a big batch of radio stations. "It was a great market," according to Dell. After a short period selling advertising, Dell got into the newspaper business and spent the bulk of her career working at several papers in the McClatchy chain before finally returning to Sacramento, where she was named publisher of the *Sacramento Bee* in 2008.

Table 6.1 Newspaper Publishers' Education

Publisher	Newspaper	Undergraduate Degree	Graduate Degree
John M. Zidich	USA Today	BA Marketing Santa Clara U.	
Robert J. Thomson	Wall Street Journal	BA Journalism Melbourne Institute of Technology	
Arthur D. Sulzberger Jr.	New York Times	BA Political Science Tufts U.	
Davan Maharaj	Los Angeles Times	BA Political Science U. Tennessee	Masters of Law Yale
Mortimer B. Zuckerman	New York Daily News	BA & BCL McGill U.	MBA U. Pennsylvania LLM Harvard
Sharon Ryan	San Jose Mercury News	BA Accounting U. Illinois	MBA Northwestern
Jesse Angelo	New York Post	BA History & Literature Harvard	
Fred Ryan	Washington Post	BA Political Science & Speech Comm. U. Southern California	JD U. Southern California
Jim Kirk	Chicago Sun Times	BS Mass Comm. Illinois State U.	
Mac Tully	Denver Post	BA Business Admin. U. Kansas	
R. Bruce Dold	Chicago Tribune	BS Journalism Northwestern	MS Journalism Northwestern
James Moroney, III	Dallas Morning News	BA American Studies Stanford	MBA U. Texas
Ed Bushey & Debby Krenek	Newsday	BS Electrical Engineering Syracuse U. BA Journalism & Marketing Texas A&M	MBA Hofstra U.
John McKeon	Houston Chronicle	BA City U. New York	
Paul C. Tash	Tampa Bay Times	BA Journalism & Political Science Indiana U. LLB U. Edinburgh	
Richard Vezza	Newark Star Ledger	BA History & Political Science Upsala College	
Michael J. Kligensmith	Minnesota Star Tribune	BA Journalism U. Chicago	MBA U. Chicago
Terrance Egger	Philadelphia Inquirer	BA Augustana College (SD)	MA Speech Comm. San Diego State U.
Timothy P. Knight	Cleveland Plain Dealer	BA Accounting Marquette U.	
Ronald C. Hasse	Orange County Register	BA Organizational Systems & Management California State U. (Northridge)	JD DePaul U.

Name	Publication	Education	
Mi-Ai Parrish	Arizona Republic	BS Journalism & Science U. Maryland	
Dennis Francis	Honolulu Star-Advertiser	Attended Edison State Community College	
John W. Henry	Boston Globe	Attended Victor Valley College U. California (Riverside, Irvine, Los Angeles)	
John F. Maher	Portland Oregonian	BA English U. Wisconsin (Milwaukee)	
Jeffrey M. Johnson	San Francisco Chronicle	BA Accounting U. Illinois	MBA U. Chicago
Brian Priester	Detroit Free Press	BS Political Science U. Central Missouri	MA Communications U. Central Missouri
Alexandra Villoch	Miami Herald	BA Political Science U. Miami	MBA U. Miami
Ray Farris	St. Louis Post Dispatch		
Michael J. Joseph	Atlanta Journal Constitution		
Craig Moon	Las Vegas Review Journal	BA Criminal Justice U. South Florida	
Frank Blethen	Seattle Times	BA Journalism Arizona State U.	
Susan Lynch Pape	San Antonio Express News	BA Accounting U. Texas (San Antonio)	
Tony Berg	Kansas City Star	BA Journalism & Strategic Comm. U. Kansas	
Trif Alatzas	Baltimore Sun	BA Communications Loyola U. (Maryland)	MA Public Affairs Reporting U. Illinois (Springfield)
Chris Stegman	Milwaukee Journal Sentinel	BA Business U. Indianapolis	
Cheryl Dell	Sacramento Bee	BA Communications California State U. (Sacramento)	
Jeff Light	San Diego Union Tribune	BA Creative Writing Brown	MBA U. California (Irvine)
John Robinson Block	Pittsburgh Post Gazette	BA History Yale	
Guy Gilmore	St. Paul Pioneer Press	BA English Literature U. California (Riverside)	
Gary Wortel	Ft. Worth Star Telegram	BA Public Relations San Jose State U.	

- A native of Boerne, Texas, a small town in the Texas Hill Country, Susan Lynch Pape earned her BA in accounting from the University of Texas at San Antonio and has spent the entirety of her professional career in that community. She held a variety of leadership positions at the *San Antonio Express-News*, the third largest daily newspaper in Texas, before becoming its publisher in 2016.
- Trif Alatzas, a native of Baltimore, grew up in what he describes as a family of "news junkies." He became acquainted with many of the people who worked for the *Baltimore Sun* because they often frequented the Bridge Restaurant, a diner his family owned, a few doors down from *Sun* headquarters on Calvert Street.

  He recalls meeting reporters and editors when he was just eight years old, washing dishes in the restaurant for his parents, "I had to stand on an overturned milk crate to reach this sink. I learned to work hard and to make sure that each plate, pot, utensil, and water glass was spotless."[9] One of those regulars gave Alatzas his first job in journalism, as an intern reporter at the now defunct *Baltimore Evening Sun*. A year later, Alatzas graduated from Loyola University, Maryland, with his bachelor's degree in communications. After stints at a variety of other news organizations, he joined the *Sun* in 2002 and became its publisher and editor in chief in 2016, the culmination of what he described as a lifelong dream to work there.
- Tony Berg was born in Emporia, Kansas, but after being adopted at a young age, moved with his family to what he refers to as the "Stanley-Olathe-Overland Park" area. He attended college at the University of Kansas, where he majored in journalism and strategic communications. After graduation, he stayed in Lawrence and took his first job at the *Lawrence Journal World*, but eventually ended up at the *Kansas City Star*, where he became the publisher in 2016, promoted from the position of vice president of advertising. Of the *Star*, Berg said, "This is the first paper I ever read, and I am going to be a good ambassador for what we do . . . that was how we got the news. I remember every day, go out to the driveway, and it was like Christmas. I've only ever worked in newspapers. I have a real passion for what newspapers stand for and what they do, and I'm still a guy that reads the physical copy of the paper every day."[10]

The resumes of the newspaper publishers reflect considerable institutional diversity. They include community colleges (Dennis Francis, of the *Honolulu Star-Advertiser*, went to Edison State Community College in Piqua, Ohio, and the *Boston Globe*'s John Henry attended Victor Valley College in Victorville, California), public regional universities (Jim Kirk of the *Chicago Sun Times* graduated from Illinois State University, *Orange County Register* publisher Ron Hasse earned his degree from California State University at

Northridge, and the alma mater of Brian Priester, with the *Detroit Free Press*, was the University of Central Missouri), and private liberal arts colleges (Terry Eggers, of the *Philadelphia Inquirer*, was a star athlete at Augustana College in South Dakota, and Chris Stegman, publisher of the *Milwaukee Journal-Sentinal*, graduated from the University of Indianapolis).

One of the publishers even graduated from what eventually became a defunct college. Richard Vezza, with the *Newark Star Ledger*, went to Upsala College and consequently owns the dubious distinction of being the only CEO in this study who graduated from a college that has gone out of business.

What They Studied

A major in one of the social sciences was the favored undergraduate course of study for the publishers with more than a third declaring a social science— political science was the leader—as their concentration, often in combination with journalism or communications as a dual major. Journalism or some kind of communications degree was the next most common major, chosen by about a quarter of the group. Business and humanities majors followed in third and fourth place, respectively. STEM majors were almost nonexistent. Ed Bushey, one of the two people sharing the publisher duties at *Newsday*, was the sole STEM graduate, majoring in electrical engineering at Syracuse University.

Graduate Studies

Fifteen of the forty-one publishers (37 percent) earned a graduate or professional degree. Among the CEO groups, this represented the lowest percentage of advanced-degree attainment, and it is consistent with the proclivity of many of these individuals to take a job with a newspaper right out of college and then stay in the newspaper business for their entire career.

Where They Studied

Two-thirds of the publishers with an advanced degree earned it from a private institution, reversing their preference for a public education at the undergraduate level. In more than half the cases, one of the top-ranked universities granted the advanced degree, with Northwestern University and the University of Chicago each granting two, and Harvard, Yale, the University of Pennsylvania, the University of Texas, and the University of California (Irvine) each granting one. An oddity of this group, for which there is no obvious explanation, is that so many of the advanced degrees—six of the fifteen—were granted by institutions located in the Chicago media market.

What They Studied

The MBA was the dominant graduate degree for the publishers, the only CEO group other than the corporate executives for which this pattern was found. Among the fifteen advanced-degree holders, seven earned an MBA and five earned an MA, most typically in journalism or another communications field. Morton Zuckerman has both an LLB and an MBA, and two publishers received a JD.

TV NEWS CHIEFS

The education of the TV news chiefs was considered separately from the editors after the discovery that the two groups had very different profiles. Had they simply been lumped into a single category, what emerged as interesting distinctions would have been missed.

Undergraduate Studies

All of the TV news executives earned an undergraduate degree, and three of them received advanced degrees. Table 6.2 summarizes the degrees for the TV news CEOs.

Table 6.2   TV Executives' Education

Executive	TV Network	Undergraduate Degree	Graduate Degree
James Goldston	ABC News	BA Philosophy, Politics, & Economics Oxford	
David Rhodes	CBS News	BA Economics & Political Science Rice U.	
Deborah Turness	NBC News	BA French & English U. Surrey	
Paula A. Kerger	PBS	BS Business Admin. U. Baltimore	
Jeffrey A. Zucker	CNN	BA American History Harvard	
Rupert Murdoch	Fox News	BA Oxford	MA Philosophy, Politics, & Economics Oxford
Philip T. Griffin	MSNBC	BA Literature Vassar College	
Justin B. Smith	Bloomberg TV	BSFS International Politics & Economics Georgetown	
Mark Hoffman	CNBC	BA Sociology U. California (Berkeley)	MA Journalism U. Missouri
Ken Jautz	HLN	BA Industrial & Labor Relations Cornell	MS Journalism Columbia

Where They Studied

The TV news chiefs tended to enroll in premier, private institutions, often located outside the United States. Thirty percent of this group went to college in another country.

- Deborah Turness, head of NBC News, graduated with a degree in French and English from the University of Surrey, a public research university in England. Born in the south of England, Turness became the first female editor of a network TV news operation in the United Kingdom when she was named the head of ITV News. In 2013, she was hired for the top spot at NBC, the latest of a number of British television executives to come to the United States to head up a news organization.
- Another British import is ABC News president James Goldston, who was educated at Oxford and began his career with the BBC in his native Britain. He won several awards for his work at ITV in England, before being lured to ABC in 2014, following Turness as the second Brit to hold the top job at one of America's three network TV operations.
- Rupert Murdoch is the founder and head of the News Corporation, a media conglomerate. He currently serves as CEO of Fox News, following the controversial and highly publicized resignation of Roger Ailes. Born in Australia, Murdoch was destined for the news business from a young age. He recalls, "I was brought up in a publishing home, a newspaper man's home, and was excited by that, I suppose. I saw that life at close range, and after the age of ten or twelve never really considered any other."[11]

  Murdoch attended Worchester College at Oxford University, where he was awarded a degree in philosophy, politics, and economics. He may not have been best known at Oxford for his academic prowess. According to one account, Murdoch was "a normal, red-blooded college student who had many friends, chased girls, went on the usual drinking binges, engaged in slapdash horseplay, tried at sports and never had enough money, no doubt due to his gambling."[12]

Of the seven TV news presidents educated in the United States, five graduated from one of the schools designated as top-ranked with Harvard, Rice, Cornell, Georgetown, and the University of California (Berkeley), each graduating one executive apiece. The other two TV news chiefs were Philip Griffin, the president of MSNBC, who received his BA in literature from Vassar College, tied for twelfth among *U.S. News* national liberal arts colleges, and Paula Kerger who earned her BS in business administration from the University of Baltimore.

What They Studied

Social science and the humanities were the majors of choice among this group, and very strongly so. Every TV news chief majored in a social science, a humanities field, or some combination of the two, except for HLN's Ken Jautz whose degree was in industrial and labor relations and the aforementioned Paula Kerger. There was not a single journalism or communications major in the bunch.

Graduate Studies

As was the case with the newspaper publishers, the majority of the TV executives did not pursue graduate education. Only three of the ten TV news chiefs have an advanced degree. Mark Hoffman (CNBC) and Ken Jautz earned master's degrees in journalism from the University of Missouri and Columbia University, respectively, and Rupert Murdoch is credited with an MA in philosophy, politics, and economics from Oxford University.

The educational histories of major news media CEOs reveal three noteworthy contrasts with the approaches taken by the other chief executive groups:

- Although 90 percent of the newspaper publishers were awarded an undergraduate degree, that is still the lowest percentage of college completion among the CEO categories. It is worth noting in passing that a number of famous TV and print journalists also succeeded at the highest levels of their trade, despite never graduating from college. The list includes Peter Jennings, Walter Cronkite, John Chancellor, Carl Bernstein, and William Safire. This trend is even more pronounced at the graduate level, with only 37 percent of the publishers and 30 percent of the television news presidents earning a graduate degree. In contrast, the majority of every other CEO group had received either a graduate or professional degree, ranging from 52 percent of the Dow 30/Fortune 500 CEOs to 100 percent for the college presidents.
- Newspaper publishers most resembled elected officials with respect to how infrequently they attended top-ranked institutions for their education. Less than a quarter attended a so-called elite institution as undergraduates, and slightly more than half did so for postgraduate study. Instead, their choice of colleges—particularly at the undergraduate level—appeared to be more influenced by factors like cost, convenience, and the opportunity to work in local media jobs that already had gotten into their blood. In the majority of instances, the pragmatics of a solid, affordable education that also enabled active learning in the workplace took precedence over institutional reputation and prestige.

The TV news presidents did not adhere to this scheme. They were much more likely, at least for their undergraduate studies, to attend highly ranked institutions, both inside and outside the United States.

• Media executives concentrated their undergraduate education in journalism, communications, and social sciences, exactly the disciplines you would predict for folks who said—as many of these leaders did—that they always knew they wanted to be journalists. At the graduate level, these CEOs also tended to focus on practical, career-serving studies, with master's degrees in journalism and the MBA being their favored degrees.

Although it is undeniably true that the news industry—whether print, digital, or televised—is becoming increasingly corporatized, the majority background of its current leaders remains grounded in fields of study like political science, history, economics, journalism, and communications, the bread-and-butter disciplines that are most relevant to the content and craft of the news itself. Journalists outnumbered accountants, history was a more popular major than marketing, and a focus on literature was more common than a concentration in management.

NOTES

1. http://www.journalism.org/2016/07/07/pathways-to-news/

2. http://www.journalism.org/2016/05/26/news-use-across-social-media-platforms-2016/

3. http://www.journalism.org/2016/06/15/newspapers-fact-sheet/

4. Ibid.

5. https://www.bloomberg.com/news/articles/2016-03-29/newspapers-gobble-each-other-up-to-survive-digital-apocalypse

6. http://www.npr.org/sections/thetwo-way/2016/12/27/507140760/big-newspapers-are-booming-washington-post-to-add-sixty-newsroom-jobs

7. http://www.journalism.org/2016/06/15/cable-news-fact-sheet/

8. http://www.csus.edu/made/dell.html

9. https://vitaminisgood.com/qa-with-trif-alatzas/

10. http://kcur.org/post/meet-new-publisher-kansas-city-star#stream/0

11. Jerome Tuccille, *Rupert Murdoch: Creator of a World Wide Empire* (Washington, DC: Beard Books, 2003), 11.

12. Ibid., 10.

Chapter 7

Presidents and Chancellors

This chapter focuses on the educational pedigrees of the presidents and chancellors of the fifty-three universities and colleges that have, throughout the book, been referred to as the nation's top-ranked institutions. Where were these leaders of our most prestigious institutions educated, and what did they study? But before we address those questions, let's learn a little more about the colleges and universities that constitute this group.

As a reminder, fifty-three institutions were defined as top-ranked based on the 2017 rankings of *U.S. News and World Report's Best Colleges.* These fifty-three institutions were divided into three groups that *U.S. News* employs in its rankings: national universities, public national universities, and national liberal arts colleges.

- A "national university" offers a full range of undergraduate programs along with a sizable array of master's and doctoral programs. Many of them operate professional schools such as law, medicine, and dentistry as well. A significant percentage of their faculty is heavily engaged in research and scholarship, often powered by the support of hundreds of millions of dollars in extramural funding from the government, business and industry, and foundations. Private universities dominate the top-tier of this category. In fact, every one of the top twenty institutions is private except for the University of California (Berkeley), which was tied for twentieth place.
- A "public national university" is very similar in scope and mission to a national university, but it is supported, at least in part, by state tax dollars,

and that subsidy allows it to charge a lower tuition to students who are residents of the state in which the institution is located than to out-of-state students. The University of California (Berkeley) is also ranked first in this group, which is where it was classified rather than with the "national" universities.

• A "national liberal arts college" focuses on undergraduate programs and offers at least half of its degrees in liberal arts fields of study. Liberal arts colleges have much smaller enrollments and a greatly reduced research mission than the institutions in the first two categories.

The top twenty institutions in the first two categories and the top ten institutions in the national liberal arts category were selected. Because of ties, fifty-three institutions ended up constituting the top fifty. The institutions are listed in table 1.2, previously.

All of the top national universities are private. Included in this group is every one of the eight Ivy League schools (Brown, Columbia, Cornell, Dartmouth, Harvard, Princeton, the University of Pennsylvania, and Yale).

Among the top public national universities, seven are the so-called Big Ten institutions, and three each are affiliated with the Pacific Ten Conference and the Atlantic Coast Conference. Six separate institutions that all are part of the University of California system claim a spot on this list, making it the only system with multiple campuses to be so recognized.

All of the top-ranked liberal arts colleges are private. Six of them are located in the New England area, two (Pomona and Claremont McKenna) are in California, Davidson is in the south, and Carleton is in the Midwest.

Clearly, the designation of only these fifty-three institutions as "top-ranked" required the imposition of arbitrary cutoffs. Had such esteemed schools as Carnegie Mellon or Tufts been added to the list of national research universities, no one would have objected too much. Likewise with the public universities, selecting the next few down in the *U.S. News* rankings like Clemson, or the University of Pittsburgh, or Rutgers would have been defensible. The top liberal arts group could have been expanded to include Washington and Lee, Colby, and Colgate and several more without degrading its perceived quality. But lines have to be drawn somewhere, and to keep this group of CEOs comparable in size to the others, this is where they were drawn.

If a defense of this list is needed, there are other subjective and objective indicators that one can point to that confirm the outstanding stature of these schools.

- Among the forty-three universities in this group, thirty-seven are members of the American Association of Universities (AAU), an invitation-only organization comprising sixty US and two Canadian universities that have long histories of preeminence as research-intensive, PhD-granting universities.
- Likewise, if we look at research expenditures, twenty of the twenty-five American universities that spend the most annually on research and development activities are included in this list.
- Of the colleges and universities with the nation's highest graduation rates, eight of the top ten are among these fifty-three schools, and as an overall group, these institutions tend to graduate a higher percentage of their students than do schools of lesser reputations.

The earlier topic of subsidies prompts the question of how much it costs to attend one of these institutions. The 2016 sticker prices for yearly tuition and fees at the national liberal arts colleges range from a low of $48,376 at Davidson to a high of $52,476 at Amherst. For the national universities, tuition and fees are the lowest at Rice University's $43,918 and the highest at Columbia with a yearly tab of $55,056. Among the top public national universities, annual tuition and fees are the cheapest for in-state students at the University of Florida ($6,389) and the most expensive at William and Mary ($18,687).

Even the unsubsidized nonresident tuition is less—often by $15,000 to $20,000 a year—at the public national universities compared to the private elites. In fact, the least expensive private school still costs more than what an out-of-state student would pay at all but two of the public institutions on the list (University of Michigan and University of Virginia). Bear in mind, however, that after taking into consideration federal financial aid and institutional scholarships, very few students pay the full price at any of these schools. Tuition is discounted for most students, often by thousands of dollars a year.

UNDERGRADUATE STUDY

All of the presidents and chancellors earned both an undergraduate degree and at least one graduate degree, the only group of chief executives to reach 100 percent at both levels. The degrees for this group are summarized in table 7.1.

Table 7.1   Presidents' and Chancellors' Education

President/Chancellor	University/College	Undergraduate Degree	Graduate Degree
Christopher L. Eisgruber	Princeton	BA Physics Princeton	MLitt Politics Oxford JD U. Chicago
Drew Gilpin Faust	Harvard	BA History Bryn Mawr	MA & PhD American Civilization U. Pennsylvania
Peter Salovey	Yale	BA Psychology Stanford	MA Sociology Stanford MS, MPhil, & PhD Psychology Yale
Robert Zimmer	U. Chicago	BA Brandeis U.	MA & PhD Math Harvard
Lee Bollinger	Columbia	BS Political Science U. Oregon	JD Columbia
Marc Tessier-Lavigne	Stanford	BS Physics McGill U. BA Philosophy & Physiology Oxford	PhD Physiology U. College London
Leo Raphael Reif	MIT	BS Electrical Eng. U. Carabobo	PhD Electrical Eng. Stanford
Richard H. Brodhead	Duke	BA English Yale	PhD English Yale
Amy Gutman	U. Pennsylvania	BA Harvard/Radcliffe	MSc Political Science London School of Economics PhD Political Science Harvard
Ronald J. Daniels	Johns Hopkins	BA Political Science & Economics U. Toronto	JD U. Toronto LLM Yale
Philip J. Hanlon	Dartmouth	BA Dartmouth	PhD Mathematics California Institute of Technology
Thomas F. Rosenbaum	California Institute of Technology	BA Physics Harvard	MA & PhD Physics Princeton
Morton O. Schapiro	Northwestern	BS Economics Hofstra U.	PhD Economics U. Pennsylvania
Christina Hull Paxson	Brown	BA Economics Swarthmore College	MA & PhD Economics Columbia
Hunter R. Rawlings III	Cornell	BA Classics Haverford College	PhD Classics Princeton
David W. Leebron	Rice	BA History & Science Harvard	JD Harvard
John I. Jenkins	Notre Dame	BA Philosophy Notre Dame BA Philosophy Oxford	Masters of Divinity Jesuit School of Theology MA Philosophy Notre Dame DPhil Philosophy Oxford
Nicholas S. Zeppos	Vanderbilt	BA History U. Wisconsin	JD U. Wisconsin

Name	Institution	Undergraduate	Graduate
Mark S. Wrighton	Washington U.	BS Chemistry Florida State U.	PhD Chemistry California Institute of Technology
Claire Sterk	Emory	Kandidaats Cultural Anthropology Free U. (Netherlands)	Doctorandus Medical Anthropology U. Utrecht PhD Sociology Erasmus U.
John J. DeGioia	Georgetown	BA English Georgetown	PhD Philosophy Georgetown
Nicholas B. Dirks	U. California (Berkeley)	BA African & Asian Studies Wesleyan U.	MA & PhD History U. Chicago
Gene D. Block	UCLA	BA Psychology Stanford	MS & PhD Psychology U. Oregon
Teresa A. Sullivan	U. Virginia	BA James Madison College at Michigan State U.	MA & PhD Sociology U. Chicago
Mark S. Schlissel	U. Michigan	BA Biochemical Sciences Princeton	MD & PhD Physiological Chemistry Johns Hopkins
Carol L. Folt	U. North Carolina	BA Aquatic Biology U. California (Santa Barbara)	MA Biology U. California (Santa Barbara) PhD Ecology U. California (Davis)
W. Taylor Reveley III	William & Mary	BA Princeton	JD U. Virginia
G.P. "Bud" Peterson	Georgia Institute of Technology	BS Mechanical Eng. & Mathematics Kansas State U.	MS Engineering Kansas State U. PhD Mechanical Eng. Texas A&M
Henry T. Yang	U. California (Santa Barbara)	BS Civil Eng. National Taiwan U.	MS Structural Eng. West Virginia U. PhD Structural Eng. Cornell
Howard Gillman	U. California (Irvine)	BA Political Science UCLA	MA & PhD Political Science UCLA
Ralph Hexter	U. California (Davis)	BA English Harvard BA Classical/Modern Languages Oxford	MA Classical & Modern Languages Oxford MPhil & PhD Comparative Literature Yale
Pradeep K. Khosla	U. California (San Diego)	Bachelor of Technology Electrical Eng. Indian Institute of Tech. (Kharagpur)	MS & PhD Electrical Eng. & Computer Science Carnegie Mellon U.
Robert J. Jones	U. Illinois	BA Agronomy Fort Valley State College	MS Crop Physiology U. Georgia PhD Crop Physiology U. Missouri
Rebecca M. Blank	U. Wisconsin	BS Economics U. Minnesota	PhD Economics MIT
Eric J. Barron	Pennsylvania State U.	BS Geology Florida State U.	MS & PhD Oceanography U. Miami
W. Kent Fuchs	U. Florida	BS Engineering Duke	Master of Divinity Trinity Evangelical Divinity School MS & PhD Electrical & Computer Eng. U. Illinois

(Continued)

Table 7.1 *(Continued)*

President/Chancellor	University/College	Undergraduate Degree	Graduate Degree
Michael V. Drake	Ohio State U.	BA African American Studies Stanford	MD U. California (San Francisco)
Ana Mari Cauce	U. Washington	BA English & Psychology U. Miami	MPhil, MS, & PhD Psychology Yale
Jere W. Morehead	U. Georgia	BA Georgia State U.	JD U. Georgia
Gregory L. Fenves	U. Texas	BS Engineering Cornell	MS & PhD Engineering U. California (Berkeley)
Mitchell E. Daniels Jr.	Purdue U.	BA Public & International Affairs Princeton	JD Georgetown
Susan Herbst	U. Connecticut	BA Political Science Duke	PhD Communication Theory & Research U. Southern California
Wallace D. Loh	U. Maryland	BA Psychology Grinnell College	MA Psychology Cornell PhD Psychology U. Michigan JD Yale
Adam Falk	Williams	BS Physics U. North Carolina	MA & PhD Physics Harvard
Carolyn A. Martin	Amherst	BA English Literature William & Mary	MA German Middlebury PhD German U. Wisconsin
Paula A. Johnson	Wellesley	BA Biology Harvard/Radcliffe	MPH & MD Harvard
Laurie L. Patton	Middlebury	BA Comparative Religion Harva'd/Radcliffe	MA & PhD History of Religions U. Chicago
Valerie Smith	Swarthmore	BA English Bates College	MA & PhD U. Virginia
Clayton S. Rose	Bowdoin	BA U. Chicago	MBA U. Chicago MA & PhD Sociology U. Pennsylvania
Steven G. Pokanzer	Carleton	BA Int'l Relations Princeton	JD Harvard
David W. Oxtoby	Pomona	BA Chemistry & Physics Harvard	PhD Chemistry U. California (Berkeley)
Hiram E. Chodosh	Claremont-McKenna	BA History Wesleyan U.	JD Yale
Carol Quillen	Davidson	BA American History U. Chicago	PhD European History Princeton

Where They Studied

The presidents and chancellors received their undergraduate education predominantly from private institutions, with thirty-four completing their degrees at a private college or university. If we break this record down further by the type of institution at which the individual serves as president/ chancellor, a modest difference emerges. Among the thirty-one heads of private institutions, twenty-two (71 percent) completed their undergraduate studies at a private school. Among the twenty-two public university leaders, twelve (55 percent) attended a private institution as undergraduates.

Attendance at a top-ranked institution was the norm, with thirty (57 percent) attending one of the other schools led by a colleague from this group. In fact, however, that percentage underestimates the extent to which this group enrolled in highly selective and esteemed colleges because it excludes some very prestigious international universities and several private colleges that enjoy outstanding reputations in the United States.

Consider that of the twenty-one presidents and chancellors of the private elite universities, eleven earned their undergraduate degrees from another top-ranked institution. As for the other ten, they include graduates of such highly regarded schools as Bryn Mawr, Brandeis, and Haverford, along with prestigious international universities like the University of Toronto, McGill University, and Vrije ("Free") University in the Netherlands.

The story is much the same with the presidents of the top ten liberal arts colleges. Eight graduated from one of the fifty-three designated top-ranked schools, and the other two attended Bates College and Wesleyan University, both of which command outstanding national reputations, ranked twenty-seventh and twenty-first, respectively, by *U.S. News.*

Among the public university leaders, eleven (exactly half) graduated from another top-ranked institution. Add in several other premier schools like National Taiwan University, Indian Institutes of Technology, Wesleyan University, Grinnell College, the University of Minnesota, and Michigan State University, and more than 75 percent of this group attended indisputably cream-of-the-crop institutions that are highly selective in their admissions, high-powered in their scholarly research, or both.

Harvard topped the undergraduate list with seven graduates, followed by Princeton with five, Stanford with three, and then Duke, the University of Chicago, and two "nonelites"—Wesleyan University and Florida State University—all with two graduates apiece.

What They Studied

The undergraduate majors of these leaders are different from other CEO groups in a couple of ways. First, none of the presidents/chancellors majored in a business field or the field of education, the only CEO group where that was the case.

Instead, they were relatively equally divided among STEM majors (38 percent), the humanities (33 percent), and the social sciences (29 percent). Engineering was the most frequent discipline, followed closely by history, English, and physics in that order.

GRADUATE STUDY

Where They Studied

Thirty-six (68 percent) of the presidents and chancellors took their terminal degrees from private institutions, the highest percentage of any CEO group. But the implications of that number are outweighed by the fact that forty-three of these individuals—an astounding 81 percent—earned their terminal degrees from one of the other top-ranked institutions. Once again, that statistic lends itself to a bit of misinterpretation because it arbitrarily excludes several renowned international institutions, all of which would be on almost any credible list of the best universities in the world.

Eighteen of the private university presidents/chancellors earned their most advanced degree from another institution in the top-ranked group. And the three who did not? They all happened to be graduates of prestigious international universities—Oxford University, University College London, and Erasmus University in the Netherlands.

For the twenty-two public university presidents, fifteen received their terminal degrees from one of the other top-ranked universities. Not to worry about the other seven. No slouches there either. Five of them were awarded graduate degrees from an AAU institution, and the other two attended the highly respected University of California at San Francisco Medical School and the University of Miami, which offers a top ten in the nation oceanography program—the specialization of alumnus and Penn State president Eric Barron.

How about the presidents of the liberal arts colleges? It's the same story. No outliers. Every one of them earned a doctoral or professional degree from an elite university.

Yale University led the list of graduate school alma maters, granting doctoral or law degrees to seven individuals. It was followed by Harvard with six, the University of Chicago with four, and the University of Pennsylvania and Princeton University, each with three graduates. Six more institutions claim two graduates each—Columbia, Georgetown, Cal Tech, the University of Virginia, the University of California (Berkeley), and the University of Wisconsin.

What They Studied

Overwhelmingly the preferred advanced degree for this group of executives is the PhD, awarded to forty-one (77 percent) of them, a rate that is more than three times greater than the next closest group, which is the foundation CEOs at 22 percent. Of course, about a third of the foundation heads had themselves been in academia, so this rank order of doctoral degree attainment is to be expected.

The JD came in second, earned by ten (19 percent) individuals. Wallace Loh, president of the University of Maryland, earned both a PhD and JD. The MD was the highest degree for only two presidents—Michael Drake at Ohio State University and Paula Johnson at Wellesley College. In addition, one president—Mark S. Schlissel, the president of the University of Michigan—earned both an MD and a PhD.

Only one person—Clayton Rose, president of Bowdoin—earned an MBA, and that was not his terminal degree. In other words, the MBA was not the terminal degree for a single president or chancellor, an unmistakable indicator of this degree's irrelevancy for the particular CEO cohort.

STEM concentrations were the most popular for the PhD, with seventeen of the presidents and chancellors completing their dissertations in those fields. Among the STEM degrees, engineering, physics, and chemistry were the most common. A social science was the focus of thirteen presidential/chancellor PhD holders, with psychology, economics, and sociology the leaders among that group. Eleven presidents took their degrees in the humanities, with history and literature being the most popular fields for them.

Academicians recognize an informal hierarchy—a professorial pecking order—of disciplines to which they pay varying levels of respect. Whether these preferences reflect prejudice or discernment is debatable, but within the academy there has been a long history of revering certain fields of study above others. Those subjects enjoying most favored status are basic sciences like physics, chemistry, engineering; core humanities like history, English, and the classics; and the more quantitative social sciences like economics and psychology. Interdisciplinary fields, education, fine arts, and applied sciences tend to fall lower on the academic totem pole.

The educational backgrounds of the presidents and chancellors reflect these internal norms. Their pedigrees are to be found largely in the most prestigious and historically honored disciplines, those scientific and humanities fields that have long conveyed authority, privilege, and credibility within the walls of academia. For someone aspiring to climb the academic ladder to a college presidency, a faculty appointment in one of these fields is a very good starting point.

In fact, that is just how most of our higher education CEOs began their careers. They received an initial faculty appointment, progressed through the tenured ranks, accepted an appointment to become a department chair, assumed the deanship of a college, and as a final preparation for a presidency became a provost, or chief academic officer, at an institution.

This was the path for Peter Salovey, who spent his entire career at Yale, and also for Nicholas Zeppos, who rose through the ranks at Vanderbilt. Likewise, Jere Morehead served in a number of faculty and administrative posts at the University of Georgia before becoming its president, and Ana Mari Cauce did the same thing at the University of Washington.

In other instances, the step-by-step march to a presidency began at one elite institution before culminating with a promotion to lead another one. Examples include Christina Paxson, who spent fifteen years at Princeton and was then named president of Brown University, and Carol Quillen, who became the president of Davidson College after serving more than twenty years in a series of positions at Rice University.

For all the currently fashionable talk about "going outside the academy" to hire university presidents, that strategy was much more the exception than the norm with this particular cohort. Mitch Daniels, former director of the Office of Management and Budget and the two-term governor of Indiana, is the only university president in this cohort to have come to the post directly from a position outside the academy.

Rebecca M. Blank, the chancellor of the University of Wisconsin is something of an "in betweener." She came to Madison directly from the job of acting secretary of the Department of Commerce, a department in which she had held a variety of important posts during a four-year period. However, most of her career was in academia in a succession of elite universities, including Northwestern, Princeton, and almost a decade at the University of Michigan, where she was dean of the Gerald R. Ford School of Public Policy.

We could also add the name of Janet Napolitano to this short list. Although she does not serve as the CEO of a campus, she is the president of the University of California system, which includes six institutions among the top-ranked public national universities. Prior to becoming the California system president, Napolitano was elected to two terms as the governor of Arizona, and she served as the Secretary of Homeland Security under President Obama.

Other than those few individuals, all of these university leaders were promoted from another academic position to the presidency or chancellorship they currently hold. This is a remarkable "insider" succession pattern, unlike anything we see with the other chief executive groups, but for the obvious exception of the military, where all the general officers are promoted from lower ranks within the armed services.

Describing the presidency of an elite university as typically an "insider's" job really does not do justice to the degree that the leadership of such institutions is inbred. Call it "an academic merry-go-round." Call it "keeping it in the family." Call it "insular," "a closed society," "clubby," or "a revolving door." The fact is that being picked to be the president of one of America's top-ranked colleges is tribalism at the highest level.

Start with the twenty-one presidents and chancellors of the top-ranked national universities, all of which are private institutions. Nine of those presidents were promoted from within their home universities, usually from the office of provost.

Of the other twelve, eleven were hired away from one of the other elite universities. The sole exception was Marc Tessier-Lavigne, who was hired to be Stanford's president after he served for five years as president of Rockefeller University, one of the world's most prestigious scientific institutions, exclusively specializing in graduate education in the medical and biological sciences and therefore in a different category than the national universities.

Now consider the academic heritage of the eight Ivy League presidents. Four were inside hires (Salovey at Yale, Eisgruber at Princeton, Faust at Harvard, and Rawlings, interim president at Cornell). The other four played a game of elite musical chairs: Columbia president Lee Bollinger came from being president of the University of Michigan. The University of Pennsylvania's Amy Gutmann was previously Princeton's provost. Dartmouth president Philip Hanlon had been provost at the University of Michigan. Christina Hill Paxson came to the Brown presidency from being a dean at Princeton.

Perhaps the ultimate in an Ivy tight circle is Hunter Rawlings, the interim president of Cornell University. He had previously served as Cornell's president a decade earlier. And in between that presidency and his current gig, he had done a prior stint as interim president for Cornell. That is known as going back to the well.

Next up, the top public national universities. Are their stairways to the top any more egalitarian? The short answer is yes, but only by a little bit. Of these twenty-two leaders, six were hired into their presidency/chancellorship from within their current institution. Nine more were hired away from other elite universities, where they had served as an academic administrator, usually the provost. These stepping-stones include Brown, Cornell, Columbia, Dartmouth, Purdue, and the Universities of California (Irvine), Georgia, Michigan, and Virginia.

The seven presidents/chancellors who did not professionally hail from one of the top-ranked campuses include the aforementioned Mitch Daniels and Rebecca Blank, and five men who were all administrators at outstanding universities—albeit not in the uppermost echelon—before their current appointment: Maryland's Wallace Loh who had been provost at the University of Iowa; Penn State's Eric Barron, who previously was Florida State

University's president; Illinois's Robert Jones, former president of SUNY-Albany; Pradeep Khosla, a dean at Carnegie Mellon prior to becoming president of the University of California, San Diego; and Bud Peterson, who had been chancellor of the University of Colorado before going to Georgia Tech.

Finally, and at the risk of monotony, the presidents of the top ten national liberal arts colleges make it a clean sweep. While none of these individuals was promoted from within their respective institutions, all but two were hired from faculty or administrative positions at another elite university, including the University of Chicago, Johns Hopkins, Harvard, Princeton, Duke, Rice, and the University of Wisconsin.

The two exceptions were Steven Pokanzer, who was hired as Carleton's president after serving as the president of the State University of New York at New Paltz (he is really only a partial exception, having done a prior four-year stint as chief of staff for the president of the University of Chicago), and Hiram E. Chodash, who was previously the dean of the S. J. Quinney College of Law at the University of Utah before accepting the presidency of Claremont McKenna.

The evidence points to an inescapable conclusion: the top spot at an elite university or college is not a destination that reflects upward institutional mobility. Usually, it's an inside job or a lateral transfer. Of our fifty-three presidents and chancellors, forty-three (just over 80 percent) were either internal hires or were recruited from one of the other fifty-two schools on the list.

How should this magnitude of exclusivity be understood? More importantly, what are the implications of this kind of institutional nepotism? Is the habitual hiring of presidents from within a very small circle of similarly situated, highly prestigious institutions meritocracy at its best, or is it simply cronyism to an extreme?

First, it is essential to acknowledge that these campus CEOs are an extraordinarily talented group of individuals, with most of them accumulating a record of educational leadership and scholarly achievements that would be the envy of almost anyone in higher education. They are a very accomplished crew. The question is not whether they are qualified—even superbly so—for their jobs because clearly they are. The issue is whether there are no equally qualified folks to be found at other institutions, albeit a little less vaunted on the prestige scale.

Is this what the academy means by a meritocracy? That 90 percent of the leaders of top-ranked institutions were themselves students at another elite institution? That no equivalently talented graduates of the University of Arizona, or Rutgers, or Boston University could be found? No drifters from Drexel? Not a single interloper from Indiana?

As it turns out, a similar kind of stratification takes place for faculty hiring as well. A recent study by Aaron Clauset, published in *Science Advances*, examined the backgrounds of 16,000 faculty members employed by 242 schools. Clauset found that just eighteen elite universities produced half of the computer science professors, only sixteen graduated half of all the business faculty, and a mere eight schools produced half of all the history professors. He concluded that the results revealed a "steeply hierarchical structure that reflects profound social inequality."[1]

In a related study, political scientist Robert Oprisko reviewed the academic backgrounds of 3,709 political science professors who were employed in 2012 by the nation's PhD-granting institutions. He discovered that just eleven schools accounted for 50 percent of the total; at the top of the list was Harvard, responsible for 239 professors.[2]

Are results like these evidence of nothing more or less than merit-based hiring in action? An additional finding by Clauset suggests that that is unlikely. The most elite schools still accounted for dramatically more faculty placements than universities that were just slightly less prestigious. As an example, the top ten schools produced three times more history professors than those schools ranked just behind them at eleven through twenty. It is hard to explain that magnitude of advantage for schools whose rankings differ by only small margins at the top of the hierarchy without attributing it to some degree of elitism.

At best, these practices represent safe choices, picking people you know or who are known by your mentors or colleagues. People who have rehearsed the rituals of other top-rung schools, who understand the vocabulary and speak the favored language, who even could unlock the closets where several skeletons may be hidden. People who are "in the network."

Perhaps elite institutions are just being cautious, wisely protecting their brand by hiring leaders who are well known and well heeled by their standards. Clearly, they are conservative choices, but whether intended or not, they are also likely to perpetuate a self-satisfied hegemony of top-ranked institutions that is based on an institutional imitation that mixes mutual flattery with contented group think.

Top colleges take pride in striving to be more diverse, and in terms of gender and ethnicity, they have made real progress in recent years. Record numbers of international students are enrolling in American universities, and women and minorities make up larger percentages of the faculty and student body than ever before.

Despite these efforts, the presidential leadership of our top-ranked universities and colleges does not reflect similar gains. It remains largely a white, good ol' boys club. Only five of the presidents of the twenty-two public national universities are women, and four of the twenty-one national university presidents are female. The most equal in terms of gender are the national liberal arts colleges, where exactly 50 percent of the ten presidents are women. Of the fifty-three presidents/chancellors, four are African American, two are Asian American, and one is from India. The rest are white Americans or Europeans.

These are exactly the outcomes you would expect, given a strategy that remains fixated on intensely recruiting the progeny of exclusive colleges. Students attending the highest echelon of American universities still come largely from the most affluent parts of society to the detriment of very well-qualified, low-income students who are often minorities and who disproportionately enroll in local and regional universities or community colleges that are far less expensive, but also have much higher dropout rates, than their more elite competitors.

The magnitude of this particular income disadvantage is staggering, and it starts with big differences in the application process undertaken by low-income and high-income students. Researchers Caroline Hoxby and Christopher Avery studied the college applications from high-achieving students (defined as those who scored at the ninetieth percentile and above on the ACT or SAT and who had at least an A- GPA from high school). They found that the majority of low-income, high-achieving students do not apply to a single selective college, even though these are the very institutions that are most likely to offer generous financial aid packages that could make them an affordable choice for students.[3]

The end result of patterns like this is that the percentage of low-income students that attend America's most vaunted universities is scandalously small. Results from the 2017 study by Raj Chetty and his colleagues that was cited in chapter 1 showed that among what they called the "Ivy-Plus" colleges (all the Ivy League colleges, plus the University of Chicago, Stanford, MIT, and Duke), more students come from families in just the top 1 percent of the income distribution (14.5 percent) than from the entire bottom half of the income distribution (13.5 percent). Looked at from a different angle, children from families in the top 1 percent of income are seventy-seven times more likely to attend an Ivy-Plus college compared to the children from families in the bottom 20 percent.[4]

Michael Bloomberg's recently launched American Talent Initiative is designed to combat this pattern. Bloomberg is pulling together a coalition of universities that publicly commit to having their student bodies become more socioeconomically diverse, based on the fundamental economic case that, according to Bloomberg, "America needs to have as big a pool of talented, hard-working, well-educated people it can possibly get."[5] The coalition is open to institutions with at least a 70 percent graduation rate, and the first members to have stepped up to push this effort forward include several of the fifty-three "top-ranked" public and private institutions.

An initiative by our top-tier colleges to enroll more poor and working-class students is laudable, and it may ultimately help diversify the pool from which their leadership has historically been drawn. However, the larger issue remains.

America's most highly regarded colleges and universities maintain a friendly stranglehold on the preparation and production of their own leadership. Our ivory towers may be resting on glass ceilings. They look like an oligarchy, yielding the one group of CEOs in this study where graduating from highly selective, top-ranked institutions is a near necessity if you want to make it to the chief executive office. They are the exception that maintains the rule—even if it applies to only a narrow segment of American society—that status matters, and that where you go can, in some instances, be more important than what you know.

NOTES

1. http://advances.sciencemag.org/content/1/1/e1400005
2. http://gppreview.com/2012/12/03/superpowers-the-american-academic-elite/
3. http://www.nber.org/papers/w18586
4. http://www.equality-of-opportunity.org/papers/coll_mrc_paper.pdf
5. https://www.nytimes.com/2016/12/13/opinion/make-colleges-diverse.html

Chapter 8

A Campus Guide to CEO U

Friends and acquaintances who knew about this project would usually ask the same one or two questions about the findings. "Did they all go to college?" was the first one. It was usually followed by "Which university had the most graduates?"

It was pretty obvious that the answer to the first one was going to be something like "No, but almost." And, as it turns out, that assumption was correct.

The answer to the second question was less obvious. But now, after combing through the records of these 344 executives and adding up all the degrees and pedigrees, the answer to that question has become much clearer along with several others about where and how the top CEOs in America were educated. The dimensions of "CEO U" have become better defined.

In this final chapter, we can summarize what these histories revealed and draw some conclusions about the educational backgrounds of the nation's leading chief executives. We have some answers to the questions of where they were educated and what they studied. We now have an idea if they opt for the nation's most elite colleges or are drawn, like millions of other students, to colleges because of reasons like convenience, cost, and size. We can assess the importance of advanced degrees. And we can judge the extent to which the MBA is a prerequisite for becoming a CEO.

DID THEY ALL GO TO COLLEGE?

To this question, the numbers tell a simple, stark truth. Without a college degree, the probability of becoming a CEO of the caliber of this group is vanishingly small. As shown in table 8.1, 335 (97 percent) of these 344 executives earned a college degree. Public official or private executive, civilian leader or military

Table 8.1   Undergraduate and Graduate Degrees Earned by American Chief Executives

	Undergraduate Degrees		Graduate Degrees	
	All Degrees	From Top-Ranked University	All Degrees	From Top-Ranked University
Governors	48/50	16/48 (33%)	36/50	13/36 (36%)
Mayors	47/50	13/47 (28%)	31/50	15/31 (48%)
Dow 30/Fortune 500	50/50	20/50 (40%)	26/50	15/26 (58%)
Foundation Heads	50/50	23/50 (46%)	43/50	29/43 (67%)
Military Officers	40/40	5/40 (13%)	39/40	7/39 (18%)
University Presidents	53/53	30/53 (57%)	53/53	43/53 (81%)
Publishers	37/41	9/37	15/41	8/15
TV Executives	10/10	5/10	3/10	1/3
Media Overall	47/51	14/47 (30%)	18/51	9/18 (50%)
Total	335/344 (97%)	121/335 (36%)	246/344 (72%)	131/246 (53%)

officer, corporate head or foundation director, the answer stays the same: a baccalaureate degree is all but a requirement for becoming a major CEO. This finding is confirmed by a recent study by Jonathan Wai and Heiner Rindermann of over 11,000 highly influential Americans, including Fortune 500 CEOs, federal judges, members of Congress, billionaires, and internationally powerful men and women. They found that over 90 percent graduated from college (incidentally, about half of the sample had attended what these authors judged to be an "elite" school).[1]

Americans have always been a bit ambivalent about the college educated. For the most part, they accept that a college education usually paves the way to a good life, offers solid preparation for a rewarding job, and helps guide personal discovery and maturation. But alongside that basic endorsement, many Americans indulge a streak of cynicism about the need for college, agreeing with sentiments like those of Teddy Roosevelt who once cracked, "A man who has never gone to school may steal a freight car, but if he has a university education, he may steal the whole railroad," or the anonymous skeptic who groused, "If nobody dropped out of eighth grade, who would hire the college graduates?"

Sentiments like these have a long history. America has been prone periodically to outbreaks of anti-intellectualism, and as multiple scholars have chronicled (see Richard Hofstadter's *Anti-Intellectualism in American Life* and Tom Nichols's *The Death of Expertise*), this phenomenon has not abated in recent years. If anything, it appears to have picked up steam.[2]

Even some of the CEOs in this sample have not always sounded all that sold themselves on the value of their college education. Warren Buffett admitted to students at his alma mater, the University of Nebraska, that he went to college primarily because his parents expected him to. "I have two degrees, but I don't have them on my wall, in fact I don't even know where they are."[3] Charlie Baker, governor of Massachusetts, was even more direct about his student days at Harvard. "Do I miss Harvard? Not for a second. With few exceptions . . . those four years are ones I would rather forget."[4]

Ambivalence aside, graduating from college is a clear expectation if you want to make it to the highest ranks of CEOs, and it is likely to remain that way. Absent a college degree, someone's raw genius or compelling charisma might punch an occasional ticket to the top, but such successes are few, despite the press's tendency to latch on to them as proof that the value of a college degree is overrated. For every Mark Zuckerberg, who said it "took five minutes to decide" to drop out of Harvard so he could found Facebook,[5] there are literally hundreds of CEOs whose college education was an important, even essential, stepping-stone to their current positions of leadership.

WHICH MAJORS ARE THE FAVORITES?

CEOs' selection of college majors was influenced largely by the type of enterprise they chose to enter and eventually lead. For the majority of the CEO groups, there was a discernible logic to their chosen majors that reflected the intent to develop knowledge in a field that was reasonably well aligned with their career plans. Either they knew what they wanted and how best to get there, or their studies helped steer them in the right direction. So we see that the elected officials tended to concentrate on the social sciences. Military officers focused on STEM disciplines, especially engineering and the physical sciences. And it comes as no surprise that media executives had their strongest academic roots in journalism, social sciences, and communications.

This is not to say that there were not plenty of unpredictable majors among their ranks. Governors who majored in the classics or home economics. Mayors who studied to be a nurse or a pharmacist. Generals with majors in English or agriculture. A newspaper publisher who had a degree in electrical engineering. As these examples make clear, a college major charts a direction, but that doesn't mean it never allows a detour.

The greatest diversity in undergraduate majors was found among three groups—the Dow 30/Fortune 500 CEOs, the college presidents and chancellors, and the heads of large foundations.

The largest percentage of the corporate CEOs opted for a STEM major, followed closely by some kind of undergraduate business degree. Social sciences and humanities majors were selected only occasionally.

The presidents and chancellors were a particularly eclectic crew, spreading their interests around in roughly equal numbers between STEM fields, humanities, and the social sciences. A business major was not to be found among their ranks.

The foundation heads divided their majors mostly between the social sciences and the humanities, with STEM and business concentrations being of little importance.

HOW IMPORTANT IS A POSTGRADUATE DEGREE?

The necessity of advanced education, in the form of a graduate or professional degree, depends on the type of CEO under consideration, but in general, a graduate degree has become the norm. Overall, 246 of these 344 CEOs (72 percent) received some type of postgraduate degree, a strong indicator of its importance as a credential.

How important depends on what type of CEO you aspire to be. If the goal is to become a university or college president or a four-star military commander, plan on earning a graduate degree. It is almost mandatory. You won't make it to the top of these organizations without one. If, on the other hand, you plan to head up a news business, a graduate degree is much less of an essential attainment, granted to only 35 percent of that cohort. A reasonable expectation for those planning to become media chiefs is that while a graduate degree is an advantage, it clearly is not a prerequisite.

As summarized in table 8.1, the vast majority of the foundation heads (86 percent), governors (72 percent), big-city mayors (62 percent), and Dow 30/ Fortune 500 execs (52 percent) also earned a graduate or professional degree, affirming the saliency, but certainly not the necessity, of graduate education for these chief executives.

WHICH GRADUATE DEGREES ARE PREFERRED?

The basic options for graduate degrees fell into five categories: a master's degree in an academic discipline, an MBA, a JD, an MD, and a PhD. Table 8.2

Table 8.2   Terminal Degrees Earned by American Chief Executives

	Master's	MBA	JD	PhD/ EdD	MD	MBA/ Master's	PhD/JD & PhD/ MD
Governors	2	7	24	1	1	0	1
Mayors	9	4	17	1	0	0	0
Dow 30/ Fortune 500 Execs.	4	15	6	0	0	1	0
Foundation Heads	7	5	14	11	3	2	1
Military Officers	33	4	1	1	0	0	0
Publishers & TV News Chiefs	8	7	2	0	0	1	0
Presidents & Chancellors	0	0	10	39	2	0	2
Total	63	42	74	53	6	4	4

shows the frequency with which the CEOs earned the various graduate degrees. (A note on methodology: table 8.2 lists only the terminal degrees earned by the executives. If an individual earned a master's degree in chemistry en route to being granted a PhD, only the PhD was counted. Likewise, if someone received an MBA and also happened to have earned an MD, a JD, or a PhD, the MBA was not counted as the terminal degree. Instances in which someone earned both an MBA and a master's degree were treated as a special category that reflected both degrees, as was any combination of MD, JD, and PhD degrees.)

The JD was the most common terminal degree, followed in order by a master's in an academic discipline, a PhD, an MBA, an MD, and then some combination of terminal degrees.

These data confirm a couple of obvious conclusions. First, there is no single best graduate degree that prepares someone to become a top-tier CEO. Having said that, it is the case that the JD proved to be an impressively versatile credential for these chief executives. A substantial number of them practiced law for a time right after finishing law school, but in many other instances their law degree ultimately served to open different doors, the ones to corporate offices, university presidencies, and elected office.

Various options for postgraduate study abound, and any of them can lead to success. Within each of the CEO categories examined, there were many different kinds of degrees awarded, including master's degrees in counseling, anthropology, geology, and divinity; and PhDs in social work, art history, and education.

Second, within each of the specific CEO groups, some graduate degrees are clearly more common than others. For example, while less than 25 percent of the CEOs overall earned a PhD, it was the coin of the realm for university leaders (held by 77 percent of them) and a valuable currency for the foundation heads, 24 percent of whom had been granted a PhD.

A doctoral degree was rare among every other CEO group. In fact, its ranking as the third most common graduate degree among all the CEOs is misleading, an artifact of how frequent it was among only one group—the higher education leaders. Unless your dream CEO destination is a college presidency, or perhaps a foundation head, the four to six years it will require to complete an academic doctorate is not an advisable strategy.

The MBA has often been touted as *de rigueur* preparation for chief executives. The data no longer support that status. In fact, the MBA was the terminal degree for less than 20 percent of all the chief executives, and it was the most common graduate degree for only one of the seven CEO categories—the Dow 30/Fortune 500 chiefs. Among the Dow 30/Fortune 500 group, only 32 percent had earned an MBA as their terminal degree, and even adding in those executives who earned an MBA but also earned another more advanced degree like a JD or an MD, would not appreciably change the MBA's overall ranking viz a viz the other graduate degrees.

Why did the MBA not rank higher? Given its long history and target audience of budding executives, what accounts for its underwhelming showing among these leaders?

The first MBA program was offered by Harvard University in 1908. In its traditional form, it takes two years to complete, and the basic curriculum includes required courses in accounting, finance, marketing, human resources, and management along with various electives. The preferred pedagogy of most MBA programs, and one of its defining characteristics, is the case method of study. The Harvard Business School, which pioneered its use, describes the case method this way:

> The case method is a profound educational innovation that presents the greatest challenges confronting leading companies, nonprofits, and government organizations—complete with the constraints and incomplete information found in real business issues—and places the student in the role of the decision maker. There are no simple solutions; yet through the dynamic process of exchanging perspectives, countering and defending points, and building on each other's ideas, students become adept at analyzing issues, exercising judgment, and making difficult decisions—the hallmarks of skillful leadership.
>
> When students are presented with a case, they place themselves in the role of the decision maker as they read through the situation and identify the problem they are faced with. The next step is to perform the necessary analysis—examining the causes and considering alternative courses of actions to come to a set of recommendations.
>
> To get the most out of cases, students read and reflect on the case, and then meet in learning teams before class to "warm up" and discuss their findings with other classmates. In class—under the questioning and guidance of the professor—students probe underlying issues, compare different alternatives, and finally, suggest courses of action in light of the organization's objectives.[6]

Over the years, the popularity of the MBA grew as more businesses began to identify it as a valued credential for their managers, and between 1970 and 2010, the number of MBA graduates soared. Applications for the MBA have slowed a little in the past decade or so, but the annual graduation of new MBAs still approaches 200,000, making it the most popular graduate degree in the country.

The degree now comes in all shapes and sizes. Full-time or part-time programs, accelerated programs that can be completed in a year, executive MBAs aimed at individuals who continue to work full-time jobs while completing their studies, evening and weekend programs also pitched to working adults, and boutique MBAs that focus on we've-got-just-the-niche-for-you specializations like supply chain management, entrepreneurship, homeland security, or sports management.

The MBA has been valued by students for four main reasons. First, an MBA curriculum covers many of the essential skills that business managers and leaders need to know. Second, with that diploma in hand, MBA graduates should be able to land better jobs and earn more rapid promotions than their peers without the degree. Third, an MBA is believed to carry a sizable wage premium, and the data do suggest that there is an "MBA bump" for graduates' salaries. How big that bump is and whether an MBA is the only or best way to secure it remain legitimate questions, but on average there is a demonstrable ROI (return on investment) for finishing the degree. Fourth, the MBA has been valued because it supposedly connects students to other up-and-coming leaders, building a network of colleagues who should prove helpful to them later in their careers.

Whether or not an MBA is a good long-term investment has been the topic of a heated debate for several years, but there has been a noticeable uptick in the number of skeptics who are sharply critical of the degree and its utility. The degree does appear to be losing some luster, not only among recipients but even with the faculty who teach in the very business schools that host the most prestigious programs.

Jeffrey Pfeffer, a faculty member at the Stanford Graduate School of Business, argues, "A degree has a value only if the degree is scarce, and the MBA is completely unscarce." Pfeffer goes on to add that unless a student goes to an elite school, "an MBA is a complete waste of money."[7]

Henry Mintzberg, the Cleghorn Professor of Management Studies at McGill University, and, over the years, one of the staunchest MBA critics in academia argues, "There's a role for MBAs for people who go into technical positions, like financial analysts, but other than that, anyone with an MBA should have a skull and crossbones on their forehead. It doesn't prepare them correctly and gives them the wrong impression of management. Instead, I think people should get smart, get educated, but mostly they should find a business or venture or activity that they really love and get immersed as deeply as possible before they try to create something."[8]

MBA grad Mariana Zanetti created quite a stir with her 2013 book, *The MBA Bubble: Why Getting an MBA Degree Is a Bad Idea*,[9] in which she skewers the MBA as a next-to-worthless degree that trumpets its own prestige and power, misleading students into thinking that their career successes are due to the degree rather than to the attributes and skills that got them admitted to graduate school in the first place.

No doubt, some of the recent fire aimed at the MBA reflects a larger angst about a shaky economy, corporate downsizing, geopolitical uncertainties, and lingering resentments toward those who are seen as college elites. But more fundamentally, the criticism boils down to dollars and cents. Investing in an

MBA degree may just no longer add up to the financial benefits claimed by its advocates.

Start with the basic price tag of the degree. Yearly tuition at the leading schools will run $40,000 at least. Add in the cost of books and other educational expenses, and the off-the-rack cost of an MBA at good business schools will hit $100,000; the bill will soar to the $125,000 mark at the premier schools. (In case you are wondering, the list of top-ranked business schools shows a remarkable overlap with the top-ranked national and public national universities that are referenced throughout the book.)

Then consider the forgone income incurred by stepping away from a job for two years while the degree is completed, to say nothing of other opportunity costs that will be paid while one is out of the workforce. Add it all together, and the all-in tab for an MBA can surpass $250,000. That's not chump change in anybody's book, and it's one of the main reasons why the degree has come under so much attack.

But there's another reason for the opprobrium directed at the MBA, and that is the belief that the degree has simply become dated and lost touch with the real business world. MBA programs remain focused on research and theory, the true loves of tenured faculty, but of much less value to businesses that are looking increasingly for more practically oriented training.

Businesses want leaders who are creative, who can work with a team and inspire coworkers rather than simply give directions to subordinates. They want executives who understand the threats and the opportunities of globalization and who prize diversity in their workforce. They are concerned that a preoccupation with profits and the bottom line results in the neglect of other vital subjects like ethics, social inequalities, and environmental stewardship, and they don't trust MBA programs to refocus on such matters.

Leading business schools have recognized the criticisms of the MBA and are experimenting with several curricular changes to improve their programs. They have introduced courses to foster greater collaboration among students and to promote a heightened awareness of ethics. Successful executives have been recruited to teach courses that connect classroom theory to corporate practice, and some programs now arrange for students to take brief visits to other countries to instill a greater appreciation for cultural influences. How successful these various innovations will be remains to be seen.

Returning to our 344 American executives, it's fair to say that while the MBA was one of the educational routes that proved useful for several, it was far from the first-class ticket to the top for the vast majority. Even among the Dow 30/Fortune 500 crew, the group you would expect to lean the heaviest on MBA preparation, more than two-thirds reached the top perch without it.

The degree was a viable option, but by no means a necessary achievement, for most of these top executives.

WHERE DID THEY GO TO SCHOOL?

As shown earlier in table 8.1, 121 of the 335 CEOs (36 percent) who earned a college degree graduated from one of the fifty-three colleges and universities that, on the basis of the *U.S. News* ratings, were designated as top-ranked. If we exclude the military officers from this calculation, based on the fact that so many of them attended one of the service academies and were therefore less likely to be attending as broad a range of schools as might otherwise have been the case, the percentage of graduates from top-ranked schools edges up to 39 percent.

Looking next at graduate schools, 131 of 246 CEOs (53 percent) with a professional or graduate degree earned it from one of the top-ranked universities. If we again exclude the military officers because of the highly specialized advanced training that so many of them pursued, the percentage of terminal degrees awarded by the top-ranked schools increases to 60 percent.

Between the various CEO categories, considerable variation becomes obvious. As already suggested, because of the unique educational expectations for military officers, their enrollment in top-ranked institutions was the lowest of all the groups at both the undergraduate (13 percent) and graduate levels (18 percent). University and college presidents were the most likely to attend top-ranked undergraduate (57 percent) and graduate (81 percent) schools, by pretty hefty margins in both cases.

The rest of the executives were bunched fairly tightly in the rates at which they earned degrees from the prestige institutions. The rank order of graduating from top-ranked undergraduate alma maters was foundation heads (46 percent), Dow 30/Fortune 500 execs (40 percent), governors (33 percent), media heads (30 percent), and big-city mayors (28 percent). Postgraduate degree completion rates at top-ranked institutions lined up this way: foundation heads (67 percent), Dow 30/Fortune 500 execs (58 percent), media heads (50 percent), big-city mayors (48 percent), and governors (36 percent).

The overall rates make one conclusion abundantly clear: these top-rung American executives were significantly more likely to attend top-ranked institutions for their graduate degrees than for their undergraduate education. This "graduate-over-undergraduate" difference was about 20 percent overall, and the difference held up—albeit with different magnitudes—for every single executive category.

Before discussing the implications of this pattern, let's answer the second most frequent question that was posed by curious individuals: Which institution graduated the most CEOs?

Undergraduate Institutions

Our 335 CEO college graduates attended 198 different institutions, including forty top-ranked schools, eighteen universities outside of the United States, and 140 other colleges and universities in the United States. The thirty institutions that produced three or more graduates are listed in table 8.3.

Harvard comes in at number one, with a total of seventeen graduates. In order, the rest of the institutions in the top ten are the US Military Academy (eleven), Princeton (nine), Stanford (eight), the Naval Academy (seven), Brown (six), Cornell (six), Yale (six), the Air Force Academy (six), and Wesleyan University (six). If we exclude the service academies because of their unique link to just one category of executive, Oxford (five), Dartmouth (four), Notre Dame (four), Georgetown (four), the University of Chicago

Table 8.3 Institutions Granting Three or More Undergraduate Degrees to American Chief Executives

Institution	Number of Degrees
Harvard	17
US Military Academy	11
Princeton	9
Stanford	8
US Naval Academy	7
Brown	6
Cornell	6
Yale	6
US Air Force Academy	6
Wesleyan	6
Oxford	5
Dartmouth	4
U. Chicago	4
U. North Carolina	4
Notre Dame	4
Georgetown	4
U. Pennsylvania	3
Duke	3
Northwestern	3
Bowdoin College	3
Boston College	3
Bryn Mawr College	3
U. California (Berkeley)	3
U. Virginia	3
U. Michigan	3
U. Texas	3
Texas A&M	3
Florida State U.	3
U. Kansas	3
San Diego State U.	3

(four), and the University of North Carolina (four) would, counting the ties, enter the top ten.

Of the thirty institutions with three or more graduates, seventeen were private and thirteen were public. Three private liberal arts colleges made the list—Wesleyan, Bowdoin, and Bryn Mawr.

These results are a Rorschach, sufficiently ambiguous to invite you to see in them what you want to see. On the one hand, there is persuasive evidence that becoming a top-notch CEO does not require attending a top-ranked college. For example,

- The majority of chief executives—more than 60 percent—did not receive their undergraduate degrees from top-ranked institutions.
- Top-ranked U.S. alma maters were outnumbered by middle-tier and lower-tier institutions by a ratio of more than 3:1.
- With the exception of the presidents of the top-ranked colleges, the majority of CEOs in every other group graduated from a school that was *not* on the list of fifty-three top-ranked schools.

Conversely, the data also support the claim that a degree from a top-ranked institution conveys a real advantage. Think of it as something like a collegiate Head Start for eventual bigwigs or a leg up on the leadership ladder. As examples,

- The fifty-three top-ranked institutions comprise less than 2 percent of all the degree-granting, four-year colleges in the nation, but they conferred more than a third of all the undergraduate degrees earned by these CEOs.
- The top-ranked institutions enroll about 6 percent of the 13.3 million undergraduates enrolled in US four-year institutions, yet they graduated 36 percent of these CEOs, a sixfold pick-me-up.
- Almost two-thirds (nineteen of thirty) of the schools that graduated three or more CEOs were on the top-ranked list.

Feel free to project your own favored interpretation on these results, but here's one reasonable perspective. There are many educational paths that can lead to the ultimate in CEO success, and the majority of them do not require that you graduate from a top-ranked school. The ranks of America's most influential chief executives are filled for the most part by individuals who graduated from colleges of all sizes, missions, and reputations. Land-grant universities and small colleges, municipal institutions and master's-level schools, expensive campuses and affordable ones—they all graduated more than one of the CEO stars on the list, proving the point that it's the person more than the place that ultimately matters, at least in this particular arena of success.

However, if you want to improve your odds of climbing to the CEO pin-nacle, graduating from a top-ranked college is a very good bet. These schools educated a disproportionate number of America's top executives. Although a college's prestige does not dictate its graduates' destinies, it appears to open a lot more doors, particularly to the executive suite.

Graduate Education

The 246 CEOs with advanced degrees attended 112 different institutions, including thirty of the fifty-three universities on the top-ranked list (because graduate offerings are very infrequent at the ten ranked liberal arts colleges, they were almost certain not to have produced any CEO postgraduates). Also included were five international universities, and seventy-seven other col-leges and universities in the United States.

Table 8.4 summarizes the twenty-six universities that had three or more graduates.

Harvard again tops the list, with twenty-one graduates. The rest of the top ten, in order, are Yale (fourteen); the University of Chicago (twelve); the military's specialized postgraduate colleges (which collectively had twelve graduates, counting only those individuals who did not earn a gradu-ate degree from a civilian university); Columbia (eleven); the University of Pennsylvania (eight); Northwestern (seven); New York University (six); and Georgetown University, and the University of Michigan were tied with five graduates. Seven universities produced four graduates apiece (Embry-Riddle Aeronautical University, Princeton, Stanford, the University of Virginia, the University of Texas, the University of California (Berkeley), and the Univer-sity of Wisconsin).

What was true for CEOs' undergraduate education remains true for their postgraduate degrees, but with some important qualifications. They still matriculated in many different types of institutions, but their range of chosen graduate schools was considerably narrower than the array of undergraduate institutions they attended.

We still encounter plenty of lesser known postgraduate alma maters like Oklahoma City University, Golden Gate University, the South Dakota School of Mines, the University of Puget Sound, and the University of Illinois at Springfield, but CEOs' enrollment in graduate schools is more "bunched up" in large, well-known universities than what we encountered at the under-graduate level.

To some extent this simply is because there are far fewer schools that offer professional and graduate degrees than offer the baccalaureate. Of the more than 3,000 four-year colleges in the United States, fewer than 150 grant the MD, about 200 operate law schools that are accredited by the American Bar

Table 8.4   Institutions Granting Three or More Graduate Degrees to American Chief Executives

Institution	Number of Degrees
Harvard	21
Yale	14
U. Chicago	12
Military Postgraduate Institutions	12
Columbia	11
U. Pennsylvania	8
Northwestern	7
New York U.	6
U. Michigan	5
Georgetown	5
U. Texas	4
Embry-Riddle Aeronautical University	4
Stanford	4
Princeton	4
U. Virginia	4
U. Wisconsin	4
U. California (Berkeley)	4
U. Miami	3
Duke	3
Vanderbilt	3
Johns Hopkins	3
MIT	3
U. Minnesota	3
U. London	3
U. Missouri	3
Oxford	3

Note: The military postgraduate institutions awarded more than twelve graduate degrees. The twelve degrees above include only those instances in which an officer did not also earn a graduate degree from a civilian university.

Association, and 335 are classified as doctoral universities, meaning that they confer at least twenty PhDs per year. Medical and law schools are typically part of a doctoral university, so the total number of US universities granting a PhD, an MD, or a JD is approximately 350. Those three degrees accounted for more than half of all the advanced degrees in this sample, making it clear that the options for graduate study are much more constrained than for BA and BS degrees.

However, the tighter clustering of graduate institutions probably reflects more than merely a reduction in the degrees of freedom for graduate study. The data suggest that for these CEOs the prestige of an institution mattered more at the graduate than at the undergraduate level. For every group of executives, a higher percentage earned their graduate degree compared to their undergraduate diploma at a top-ranked institution. Overall, that difference was 17 percent, but if we exclude the somewhat anomalous results for the military leaders, it grows to 20 percent.

A finer grain analysis adds more support to the greater importance of completing a graduate rather than undergraduate degree at a top-ranked school. The interaction between CEOs' undergraduate and graduate degrees and the rankings of the institutions that conferred those degrees can go in one of four directions: attending a top-ranked school for both degrees, attending a school not in the top-tier for both degrees, attending a top-ranked undergraduate school followed by a graduate school not in the top-tier and attending an undergraduate school not in the top-tier and then going to a graduate school at a top-ranked institution.

Table 8.5 shows how often each CEO group moved along one of those four paths. Several comparisons stand out. First, 40 percent of chief executives obtained both their undergraduate and graduate degrees from institutions that were not included among the fifty-three top-ranked schools, one more illustration of the finding that graduating from an elite school was not a prerequisite for these CEOs.

Second, 22 percent of the CEOs attended a top-ranked graduate school after having graduated from an undergraduate institution that was not in the top-ranked group. This rate is three times greater than the percentage (7 percent) of CEOs who reversed that direction and followed their undergraduate education at a top-ranked school with a graduate degree from a school not in the top-tier.

What accounts for this trajectory? Several explanations come to mind. Perhaps these individuals were advised and assisted by their undergraduate mentors to "up their game" and apply to more selective institutions. Or, maybe their undergraduate experiences increased their confidence that they could compete against the best and they took up that challenge on their own. An even more likely reason may be that with the maturation and

Table 8.5   CEO Pathways from Undergraduate to Graduate Institutions

CEO Type	Lower-Tier Undergraduate to Lower-Tier Graduate	Top-Ranked Undergraduate to Top-Ranked Graduate	Top-Ranked Undergraduate to Lower-Tier Graduate	Lower-Tier Undergraduate to Top-Ranked Graduate
Governors	21	10	2	3
Mayors	15	8	1	7
Dow 30/Fortune 500	7	7	4	8
Foundation Heads	12	18	2	11
Presidents/Chancellors	30	25	4	18
Military Leaders	6	1	3	5
Media Heads	8	7	1	2
Total	99	76	17	54

understanding that they gained during their college years came more self-awareness about career goals and a greater appreciation about how a degree from a top-ranked university could help advance that career.

Finally, the percentage of individuals who earned both their undergraduate and advanced degrees at top-ranked institutions (31 percent) is only marginally greater than the executives who moved from an unranked undergraduate institution to a top-ranked graduate school (22 percent). The majority of our CEOs attended a top-ranked graduate school, but they did not appear to be greatly handicapped in that pursuit by first attending a less prestigious institution for the baccalaureate degree.

To the questions of how are the nation's leading executives educated—where did they go and what did they study, here are some final thoughts.

1. In the end it is impossible to determine how big a role higher education played in the careers of these chief executives. Success has many fathers, and for this group, their individual climbs to the top were aided, in some unknown combination, by raw intelligence, emotional stability, dogged determination, ready energy, the right friends, trusted mentors, and old-fashioned good luck.

   Although we can't quantify its contribution, a college education obviously was a key factor in this mix as well. When 97 percent of a cohort claims a common achievement—in this case a college degree—in its background, it is not a coincidence, nor an accident. It is an experience that matters, so essential for these leaders that it stopped just short of being an absolute requirement.

2. These CEOs chose undergraduate majors that were all over the curricular map. Granted there were no dance, music, geography, or Russian majors in the group, but it is possible to find at least one of just about everything else. With the exception of the military leaders and the CEOs of Fortune 500 technology companies, where, in both cases, STEM degrees were predominant, a particular college major did not appear to be a leading or a limiting factor. "Major in what interests you the most" may be the best advice here, as it is in most cases.

3. Similar advice holds for advanced degrees, although if an individual has any interest in studying law, the JD seemed to have served many of these chief executives especially well. An MBA? It's no longer the passport to the promised land, if it ever was. Business and leadership consultant Tom Peters has expressed unvarnished disdain for the MBA, calling it "the Masters of Paper Pushing," while endorsing alternatives such as the Master of Fine Arts (creativity rules the marketplace), the Master of Metabolic Management (awarded to people who hustle), the Master of Madness (held by creative people who "screw around vigorously"), the Master of

Non-Masculine Leadership (because women's skills are perfect for leadership in the new economy). And the Doctor of Enthusiasm! (because enthusiasm is the greatest trait of all).[10]

4. If you have to choose for some reason between attending a top-ranked undergraduate institution or a top-ranked graduate school, pick the latter. It's where prestige seems to play the stronger hand, confirmed by the fact that more than a fifth of these CEOs attended a top-tier graduate school after graduating from a lower-tier undergraduate institution.

5. All things being equal, attending a top-ranked school brings clear benefits to aspiring executives. In addition to the formal education provided, these schools give students the chance to cooperate and compete with some extremely talented peers, sharpening the analytical and leadership skills that executives should display. They expose them to well-known and respected mentors whose stamp of approval in the form of insider tips and personal recommendations can go a long way in helping land the most coveted jobs. And they connect them with a network of social contacts that will serve them well for years to come.

   J. D. Vance captured the power of this social and family networking from a student's point of view in his autobiography, *Hillbilly Elegy*. Commenting on his job interviews as he finished up law school at Yale, Vance recalls,

   > That week of interviews showed me that successful people are playing an entirely different game. They don't flood the job market with resumes, hoping that some employer will grace them with an interview. They network. They email a friend of a friend to make sure their name gets the look it deserves. They have their uncles call old college buddies. They have their school's career office set up interviews months in advance on their behalf. They have parents tell them how to dress, what to say, and whom to schmooze.[11]

6. But, of course, all things are not equal, as the careers of these CEOs prove. Graduating from an elite college definitely improves the odds for chief executive success, and it may even help cover the spread incurred from a less-than-stellar academic record, which had it come from a lower-tier college would have been a larger handicap.

The overall moral of our story still remains clear cut: as many advantages as an elite-college education conveys, it doesn't have a corner on the market. America's leading chief executives were able to gain an education that served them well at many different colleges, not just the most selective, expensive, or prestigious ones. Instead, they graduated from the admirable diversity of institutions that has long been a hallmark of our country's higher education system.

Leading CEOs selected colleges that served their needs more than glossed up their resumes. They sometimes picked a lesser known school because a family member had gone there before them and reported a wonderful experience. They often stayed close to home so they could afford to go to school. To pay their tuition, many worked part-time jobs, sometimes at the very organizations they would later lead.

Regardless of where they enrolled, many searched out and attached to a faculty mentor, an older student, or a coach who took a special interest in them and became a trusted advisor in their lives. They threw themselves into a campus club or organization that indulged their passion and grew their confidence. They took on an internship that gave them a first inkling of what they could become, a taste of what it would be like to live the lives they had imagined.

In short, they made whatever institution they attended into what most American colleges almost always can be for students who make a genuine commitment to their education: a noble place that makes it safe to feel uncomfortable, that encourages you to change your mind, and gives guidance if you change your direction. A place that allows self-discovery as much or more than it transmits knowledge. A place that extends the chance to take risks—to fail, to succeed, and to learn from both experiences. A place that awakens dreams.

NOTES

1. http://www.tandfonline.com/doi/full/10.1080/13598139.2017.1302874

2. Richard Hofstadter, *Anti-intellectualism in American Life* (New York: Alfred A Knopf, 1963). Tom Nichols, *The Death of Expertise* (New York: Oxford University Press, 2017).

3. http://www.businessinsider.com/warren-buffett-trashes-higher-education-says-its-not-for-everyone-2012-5

4. http://archive.boston.com/news/politics/articles/2010/10/03/baker_happy_days_high_expectations/?page=3

5. http://fundersandfounders.com/entrepreneurs-who-dropped-out/

6. http://www.hbs.edu/mba/academic-experience/Pages/the-hbs-case-method.aspx

7. https://www.ft.com/content/2313a2f8-7c81-11e3-b514-00144feabdc0

8. https://www.entrepreneur.com/article/224440

9. Mariana Zanetti, *The MBA Bubble: Why Getting an MBA Degree Is a Bad Idea* (Charleston, SC: Create Space Publishing, 2013).

10. http://www.businessmanagementdaily.com/7300/peters-candidates-to-replace-the-mba

11. J. D. Vance, *Hillybilly Elegy: A Memoir of a Family and Culture in Crisis* (New York: Harper Press, 2016).

About the Author

Dr. Michael T. Nietzel currently is the deputy director of the Missouri Department of Mental Health. From 2010–2016, he served as the senior policy advisor to Governor Jay Nixon, where he focused on the areas of education, mental health, international trade, and workforce development. Prior to these positions, Nietzel was the ninth president of Missouri State University, beginning in 2005 and serving until his retirement in 2010.

Nietzel came to Missouri State from the University of Kentucky, where he had held a number of academic positions over a thirty-two-year period. He joined the faculty at Kentucky in 1973 as an assistant professor of psychology. From 1977–1990, he served as director of the Clinical Psychology Training Program, and in 1991, he was named chair of the Department of Psychology, completing a second term as chair in 1997. In 2002, he was named provost of the University of Kentucky. Prior to being provost, he served as dean of the Graduate School for four years. He was awarded an honorary degree by the University of Kentucky in 2013.

He received his BA from Wheaton College in 1969, and his MA in 1972 and his PhD in 1973 both from the University of Illinois.

www.ingramcontent.com/pod-product-compliance
Lightning Source LLC
Chambersburg PA
CBHW021601210326
41599CB00010B/553